U0467569

© Peyo

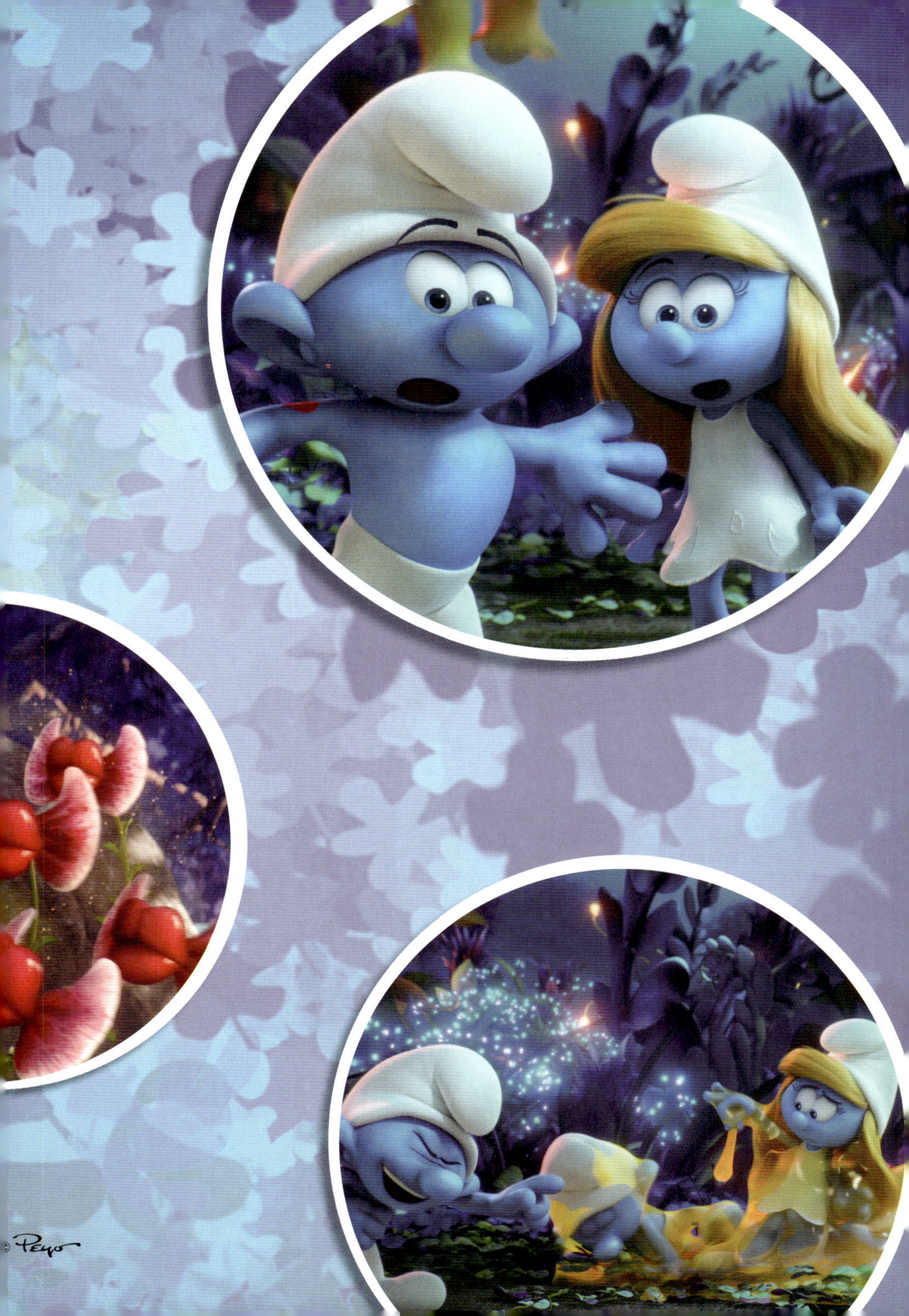
© Peyo

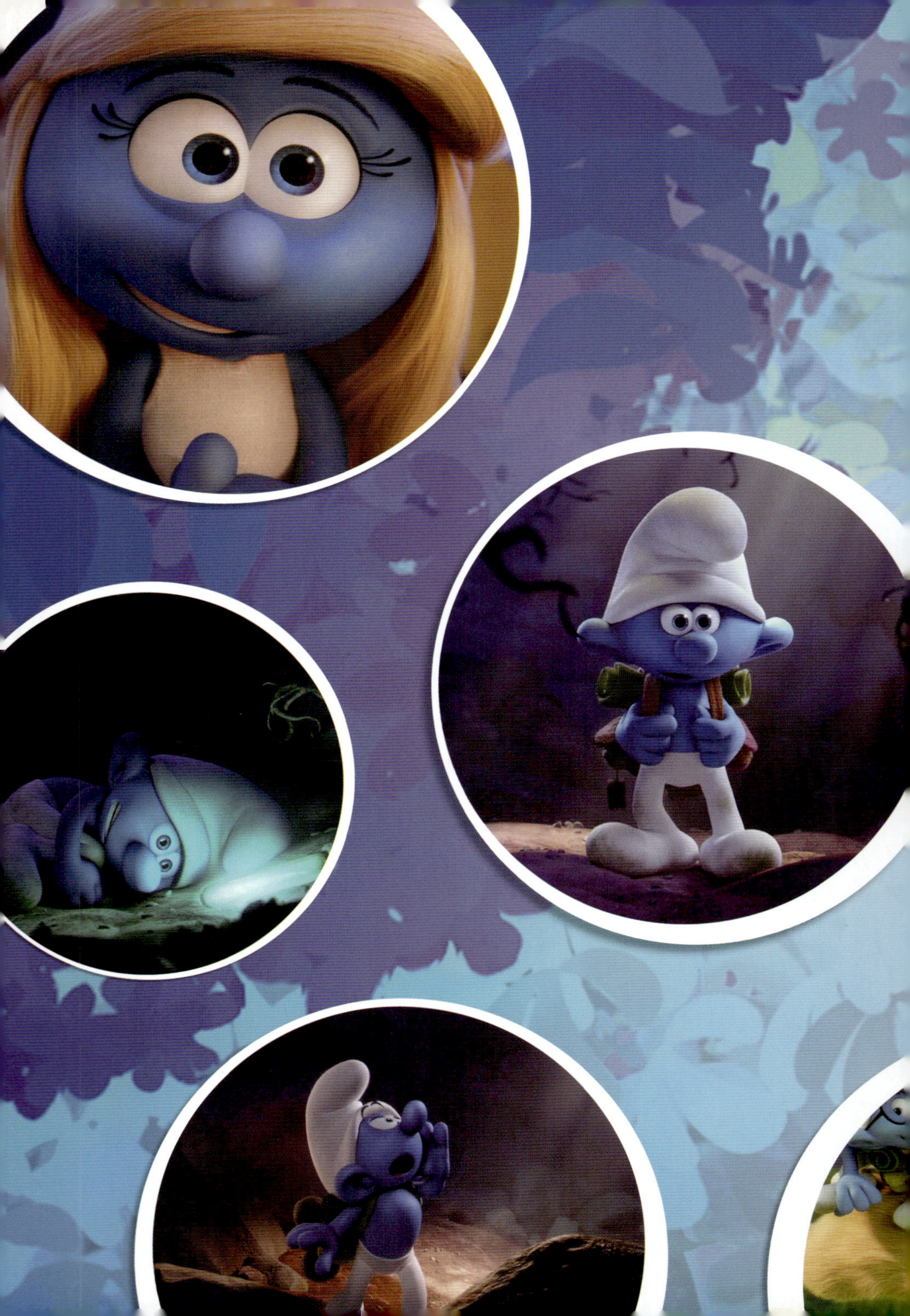

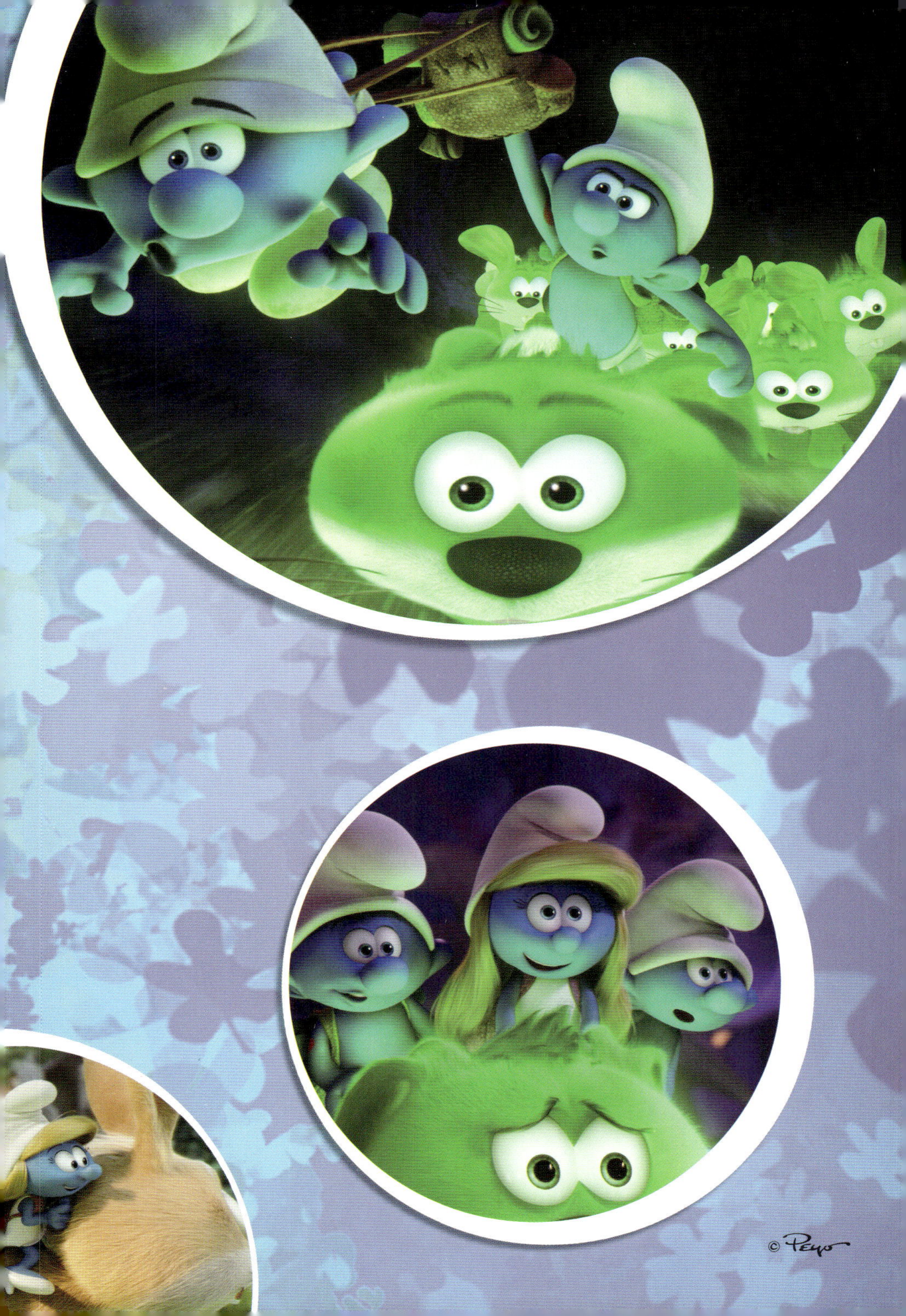
© Peyo

© Peyo

THE LOST VILLAGE

探寻神秘村

[美]斯塔西亚·多依奇 著　刘婧，张俊 译

© 中南博集天卷文化传媒有限公司。本书版权受法律保护。未经权利人许可，任何人不得以任何方式使用本书包括正文、插图、封面、版式等任何部分内容，违者将受到法律制裁。

著作权合同登记号：图字18-2018-022

© Peyo - 2018 - Licensed through I.M.P.S. (Brussels) - www.smurf.com
Movie novelization bilingual (Chinese and English) © Peyo 2018,
Translation: © Peyo
Chinese and English bilingual edition ©China South Booky Culture Media CO,LTD
All rights reserved.

图书在版编目（CIP）数据

探寻神秘村 /（美）斯塔西亚・多依奇著；刘婧，
张俊译. — 长沙：湖南少年儿童出版社，2018.9
　（蓝精灵经典小说：中英双语版）
　ISBN 978-7-5562-3885-9

　Ⅰ.①探… Ⅱ.①斯…②刘…③张… Ⅲ.①英语—汉语—对照读物②儿童小说—长篇小说—美国—现代
Ⅳ.①H319.4：I

中国版本图书馆CIP数据核字（2018）第156801号

LANJINGLING JINGDIAN XIAOSHUO ZHONGYING SHUANGYU BAN
TANXUN SHENMI CUN
蓝精灵经典小说中英双语版・探寻神秘村
[美]斯塔西亚・多依奇　著　刘婧　张俊　译

责任编辑： 阳　梅　李　炜		**策划出品：** 小博集
策划编辑： 姬亚楠		**特约编辑：** 廖若星
营销编辑： 李　秋		**版权支持：** 文赛峰
版式设计： 云朵儿		**封面设计：** 李　洁

出版人：胡　坚
出版发行：湖南少年儿童出版社　　　　　　　地　　址：湖南省长沙市晚报大道89号
邮　　编：410016
电　　话：0731-82196340（销售部）　　0731-82194891（总编室）
传　　真：0731-82199308（销售部）　　0731-82196330（综合管理部）
常年法律顾问：湖南云桥律师事务所　　张晓军律师
经　　销：新华书店　　　　　　　　　　　　印　　刷：北京尚唐印刷包装有限公司
开　　本：880 mm×1270 mm　　1/32　　　印　　张：7
版　　次：2018年9月第1版　　　　　　　　印　　次：2018年9月第1次印刷
书　　号：ISBN 978-7-5562-3885-9　　　　定　　价：28.00元

若有质量问题，请致电质量监督电话：010-59096394　　团购电话：010-59320018

目录
CONTENTS

第1章　蓝妹妹的苦恼　　　　　　　　　　001

第2章　蓝精灵特性探测器　　　　　　　　008

第3章　蓝妹妹被抓走　　　　　　　　　　012

第4章　格格巫的邪恶计划　　　　　　　　019

第5章　蓝精灵小队的秘密行动　　　　　　029

第6章　走进禁忌森林　　　　　　　　　　035

第7章　掉进兔子窝　　　　　　　　　　　042

第8章　生火、露营、扎筏　　　　　　　　049

第9章　格格巫的骗局	057
第10章　来到神秘村	062
第11章　格格巫逃离沼泽	072
第12章　格格巫突袭蓝精灵果园	082
第13章　蓝妹妹营救蓝精灵（1）	090
第14章　蓝妹妹营救蓝精灵（2）	095
第15章　齐聚精灵村	100

Chapter 1 Smurfette in Distress	105
Chapter 2 Smurfy Thing Finder	113
Chapter 3 Smurfette was Captured	118
Chapter 4 Gargamel's Evil Plan	125
Chapter 5 Secret Action of Team Smurf	136
Chapter 6 Entered the Forbidden Forest	143
Chapter 7 Inside the Rabbit Warren	151
Chapter 8 Started Fire, Camped out, Built Raft	159
Chapter 9 Gargamel's Scam	167
Chapter 10 Arrived in the Lost Village	173
Chapter 11 Gargamel Ran Away from Swamp	184
Chapter 12 Gargamel Attacked the Smurfy Grove	195
Chapter 13 Smurfette Saved Smurfs (1)	203
Chapter 14 Smurfette Saved Smurfs (2)	208
Chapter 15 Gathered in Smurf Village	213

第1章　蓝妹妹的苦恼

"许多伟大的冒险通常都是从有趣的地方开始的。比如，这个冒险故事就发生在森林深处的一个神秘地方。欢迎来到精灵村！在这里，所有的蓝精灵都在古朴的蘑菇屋里快乐地生活着。"蓝爸爸抬起头，视线从手中的书移向窗外，精灵村此时正呈现出一派忙碌热闹的景象。"哦，你想问蓝精灵长什么样？好吧，先来个小小的背景介绍吧。"

就在这时，一个蓝精灵飞快地跑进村子，一路上撞到了所有能撞到的人和东西。

这就是一个完美的例子。"好，现在来了一个蓝精灵。蓝精灵们都是小小的个子，有着蓝色的皮肤，戴着滑稽的帽子。他们穿着白色的紧身裤，看起来漂亮极了。蓝精灵们平时会干什么呢？只要问问他的名字就知道了。例如，这位叫作笨笨。"蓝爸爸说完，会心一笑。

"嘿！"笨笨挥手打着招呼，压根儿没看路。果不其然，他被绊倒在地，摔了个跟头，栽进了一截空心木头里。

"我没事！"笨笨的声音在村里回荡。

蓝爸爸微微一笑，摇了摇头，继续介绍下去。

"接着，这两位是乐乐和蒙蒙……"

* 探寻神秘村 *

乐乐递给蒙蒙一个礼物盒子。"给你的礼物！"乐乐喊道。突然，盒子爆炸了，乐乐哈哈大笑。

"跟你开个玩笑。我本来是想给你这个。"乐乐说着，拿出了另一个盒子。

"哇，谢谢！"蒙蒙开心地接过礼物，但当他打开盒子时，一个拳击手套弹了出来，狠狠地打中了他的脸。

在村子另一头，健健正在做俯卧撑。

"98，99……100！"他哼了一下，亲吻着自己健硕的肱二头肌，"接下来是单指俯卧撑！"

"这边是书呆子蓝精灵。"蓝爸爸指着一个踩着滑板车经过的蓝精灵说。

"你叫我什么？"这个蓝精灵回过头来，瞪着蓝爸爸。

"对不起，聪聪。开个玩笑！"聪聪踩着滑板车继续前行。"还有剧剧和唆唆。"

"看这个！"唆唆坏笑着说。"嘿！当心！"他冲着剧剧喊道。

剧剧突然撞上了一堵隐形的墙。

"呃……那边发生了什么事？"奇奇大声问。

奇奇一直在用望远镜观察着一切。他发现兢兢迅速拉上了窗帘。

"还有赢赢和输输……"蓝爸爸指着两个正在下棋的蓝精灵说。赢赢获胜了，他正要庆祝，输输则一气之下掀翻了棋盘。

第1章 蓝妹妹的苦恼

"道道。"蓝爸爸冲一个蓝精灵挥手,那个蓝精灵一脚踢在蒙蒙的肚子上。

灵灵正在钉钉子。

浮浮正在陶醉地照着镜子。

农农正在他的花园里摘萝卜。

画画正为他的杰作收尾。

焙焙烤好了一个蛋糕。

明明把这个蛋糕变没了。

还有更多的蓝精灵呢:潜潜、警警、医医、"吃桌子的蓝精灵"……

蓝爸爸顿了一下,承认道:"是的,我们对最后这位蓝精灵也不是很了解。"他耸了耸肩说:"然后是我——蓝爸爸。我穿着红色的紧身裤。"蓝爸爸说完笑了,由于笑得太厉害,肚子都抖了起来。接着蓝爸爸突然严肃起来。"但这个故事不是关于我的,也不是关于他们的。这是她的故事。"

屋外,一位肩披金色长发、身着白裙子的蓝精灵从蓝爸爸的窗前经过。"蓝妹妹。"蓝爸爸笑着说,"我们村里唯一的女孩。"

蓝妹妹走过村子时,其他蓝精灵都高兴地和她打招呼。

"嘿,净净!"蓝妹妹冲他挥手,然后向另一群蓝精灵挥手,"大家好!"

蓝爸爸靠在椅子上。"但这不是蓝妹妹与其他蓝精灵唯一不同的地方。"他解释说,"蓝妹妹是邪恶的巫师格格巫创造出来的,他通过黑暗魔法用一块黏土捏出了蓝妹妹。"

在精灵村上方的半山腰处,有一座破败的城堡矗立在布满岩石的山崖边。那座城堡肮脏简陋,孤零零的,那里的天气总是很糟糕,黑暗的天空中布满了闪电,雷鸣声不绝于耳。

在阴暗的废墟里面,邪恶的巫师正将蓝色黏土捏成一个蓝精灵的模样。他挥动魔杖,使用黑暗魔法为黏土注入生命。

砰!一道月光直射在黏土上,一个邪恶的蓝妹妹从烟雾中站了起来。这个蓝妹妹和现在住在精灵村里的那个蓝妹妹完全不同。她露出了阴险的笑容。

蓝爸爸打了一个寒战。"起初,蓝妹妹和格格巫一样坏。巫师派蓝妹妹去寻找精灵村,让蓝妹妹帮助他抓住我们所有人。"

邪恶的蓝妹妹进入了村子,她只有一个目标:在村子里搞破坏。

"幸运的是,我自己对魔法也略知一二,并且我能够找到蓝妹妹身上善良的一面,帮助她把善良的一面发扬光大。"蓝爸爸说。

善良的蓝妹妹花了一点时间适应新的自己,等她做到后,她成了每一位蓝精灵的朋友。

蓝爸爸把手放到膝盖上的故事书上。"但是现在还有一个问题。我们没有办法通过'蓝妹妹'这个名字了解她的特点。"

蓝妹妹曾试着和聪聪一起做化学试验,结果并不好,聪聪最

第 1 章　蓝妹妹的苦恼

后掉进了一个洞里！她曾拜道道为师学习空手道，但是当她踢到他时……呃，我们只想告诉你，穿着高跟鞋踢人确实非常疼！

"她的名字没有告诉我们她是怎样的人，或者她的特点是什么。那么，蓝妹妹到底是什么样的呢？"

这真是一个大问题。每个人都想知道答案。

蓝妹妹试着和焙焙一起烤蛋糕，结果蛋糕变成了碎屑。焙焙的结论是："好吧，她不是面包师，这点我可以肯定。"

聪聪从他丰富的藏书中找出了蓝精灵指南，并开始翻阅。"嗯，让我们看看。蓝妹妹……蓝妹妹……呃，书里没有。"

"你知道……一个蓝妹妹的……呃……"灵灵什么也想不出来。

农农同样也糊涂了。"这个，天哪，这个问题真难答。"

剧剧只是耸了耸肩。

"'蓝妹妹'是什么意思呢？"邮邮仔细想了想答案，"呃，她是，呃，她是……呃。"

健健有了答案，他笑着说："她是最伟大的……"

浮浮仍然陶醉地照着镜子，说："地球上最令人惊奇的生物！就是你！"他指的是他自己，而不是蓝妹妹。"不好意思，你问我什么来着？"

"蓝妹妹？呃……哦！我懂了！"笨笨是她最好的朋友之一。他说："这是一个我们永远不会知道答案的问题！"笨笨不知道的是，蓝妹妹听见了他们所有人的回答，她发现大家都觉得她很奇怪。这让蓝妹妹感到很伤心。

探寻神秘村

经过深思熟虑后,蓝爸爸再次提出了这个问题:"那么,'蓝妹妹'究竟是什么意思?"他耸了耸肩,"没有人比蓝妹妹更渴望知道这个问题的答案了……"

爵爵演奏了一首悲伤的乐曲,而蓝妹妹到处闲逛,最后走到一个长凳前坐下。她叹了口气,看着周围的一切。

"呃,你在干什么呢?"厌厌站在长凳旁,不停地围着蓝妹妹转圈。

"哦,嘿,厌厌。我只是刚好要……"

"离开。"这是厌厌的建议。

"呃……"蓝妹妹可没打算这样做。

"这是我的长凳。我每天都在同一时间来到这里……"

"噢,让我猜猜……"她打断厌厌,"来发牢骚。"

"是的。"

蓝妹妹坐到另一边,让厌厌坐到她旁边。

"我也可以做到,我会发牢骚。"她试图模仿厌厌的声音和语调。

一个蓝精灵经过他们身边。"嘿,厌厌。嘿,蓝妹妹!天气真好啊,是吧?"

"不,压根儿不是!"厌厌毫不掩饰自己的性格。

"马上要下……雨啦!"蓝妹妹抱怨着,但听起来不太对。她不是一个天生爱发牢骚的人。她用自己的声音接着说:"这实际上有助于植物生长!"她试着再抱怨一次:"但也意味着马上

第 1 章　蓝妹妹的苦恼

要乌云密布了！所以，仔细想想吧！"她接着又说："但是那之后也可能会有彩虹！"保持发牢骚的状态可真难！"不过彩虹看起来很蠢！"

蓝妹妹摇了摇头。她就是无法做到。"开玩笑，我喜欢彩虹！哈哈！"

"事实上，你不是很擅长发牢骚，我说的没错吧？"厌厌带着抱怨的口吻叹了口气。

"呃，是的，我不擅长。"她承认。

"事实上，你的牢骚还很烂。"厌厌仍然是村子里唯一爱发牢骚的蓝精灵。

"是的。"蓝妹妹起身离开，没走多远又停下脚步，回过头来。

"但你发的牢骚也很烂！"哦，这么说真可怕。"我撒了谎！你真的非常、非常善于发牢骚！"

最后，只有一件事可以肯定：蓝妹妹仍然不知道做一个蓝妹妹意味着什么！

第2章　蓝精灵特性探测器

蓝妹妹来到聪聪的蘑菇屋前。正当她要敲门的时候，聪聪突然打开门。他穿着一件实验服，看起来很疲惫。

"嘿，聪聪！"蓝妹妹高兴地说。

聪聪咳嗽了一下。"啊，蓝妹妹！你能来真是太棒了！"他探出头，紧张地看了看周围，然后抓住蓝妹妹的手臂把她拖进了屋。

蓝妹妹想抗议："我正准备……哇！"在聪聪的实验室里，健健正坐在椅子上，头上戴着一顶可笑的帽子。这顶帽子是用老式意大利面漏勺和一些根茎类蔬菜做成的，还通过电线连到一台嘎嘎作响的机器上。

"我们正在对我的新发明——蓝精灵特性探测器进行测试。测试目标：健健。"聪聪向蓝妹妹解释。

"嘿，蓝妹妹。"健健挥手跟蓝妹妹打招呼。

"呃……嘿，那东西是安全的吗？"蓝妹妹小声问聪聪。当她看到聪聪退到一个防爆护盾后面时，蓝妹妹更加担心了。

"安全吗？"聪聪对蓝妹妹的担心毫不在意。"噗！当然。"他顿了一下，深吸了一口气，警告蓝妹妹说，"不过如果我是你的话，我会到这后面来。"

第2章 蓝精灵特性探测器

蓝妹妹想了一下,决定和聪聪一起躲到防爆护盾的后面,让健健一个人留在椅子上。聪聪让他的"拍拍虫"记录测试过程。拍拍虫相当于蓝精灵的智能手机,不同的是,拍拍虫也是一只真正的瓢虫。

"拍拍虫,开始记录。蓝精灵特性探测器,测试实验1.03。"他抬起头问健健,"准备好了吗,健健?"

"没问题!"健健竖起大拇指。

仪器启动了,运行速度设为最大。伴随着一连串丁零声和哨子声,帽子和预测转盘之间闪烁着一串电光。转盘疯狂地转动,最后停在一个图标上,是一张画有健硕的肌肉手臂图片。

"哇!"蓝妹妹惊讶地屏住了呼吸。

"哈哈!测试成功了!"聪聪欢呼起来。

拍拍虫也跟着一起庆祝。

"哇!这玩意儿真懂我。"健健说着,曲肘摆出健美的姿势。

聪聪告诉蓝妹妹:"它可以找到健健的显性特征……"

"超级强壮!"健健开心地边说边亲吻他的肱二头肌。

"并把它提取出来,"聪聪举起一个饮料罐,"我称它为'聪聪牌超级蓝精灵能量饮料'。"他把饮料罐递给蓝妹妹。"给你,你可以第一个试用!"

蓝妹妹仔细地端详着"能量饮料",拿不定主意是否要试用。

聪聪连忙跑开,跳到防爆护盾后面。"警报解除!"他喊道,意思是说蓝妹妹可以喝了。

蓝妹妹摇了摇头。"你看,听到你说'警报解除',我就立马不想喝了。"

这时候,蘑菇屋的门猛地被推开,笨笨冲了进来。

"嘿,伙计们!"他把饮料从蓝妹妹的手中撞飞了出去,然后砰的一声,饮料爆炸了,把墙面炸出了一个大洞,还冒着烟呢。

哟!蓝妹妹庆幸自己刚才没有喝下去!

"嘿,笨笨!"他们异口同声说道。

"你正好赶上见证科学的历史时刻。"聪聪说道。他抬起头,透过爆炸留下的空洞,看到奇奇晃晃悠悠地经过,奇奇正想知道里面发生了什么事情。

"这儿发生什么事了?"奇奇一边问一边不停地打量着屋里的一切。

聪聪、健健、蓝妹妹和笨笨异口同声地说:"不关你的事,奇奇!"

"嗯,好吧,好吧。"奇奇没觉得生气,继续走他的路。

突然,蓝妹妹有了一个主意!也许现在她终于可以知道她的名字意味着什么了!"嘿!如果那顶蔬菜帽子可以测试出健健很强壮,也许它也能告诉我'蓝妹妹'的本质是什么。"她冲上前戴上奇怪的帽子。"开始吧,聪聪!"

聪聪启动机器,其他男孩都躲到防爆护盾后面。

聪聪按下开关,仪器又发出了一串丁零声、哨子声,机器运

第 2 章　蓝精灵特性探测器

行了一会儿，突然冒出火花和烟雾，帽子上的灯光灭了，然后开始不停地抖动起来。整个蘑菇屋发出一阵隆隆声。蜡烛熄灭了。聪聪家所有的家具都像被磁铁吸引一样朝蓝妹妹移动过去，最后蓝精灵特性探测器在一阵噼里啪啦声中停止了工作，帽子上的蔬菜也都枯萎了。

"哇！"聪聪大喊，从防爆护盾后面出来，"太神奇了！"

"怎么回事？！"蓝妹妹感到困惑，为什么机器没有像对健健那样有效？

"不知道因为什么，你的能量没有散发出来。相反，你吸收了周围的能量。很可能是因为你不是一个真正……"聪聪突然意识到了什么，啪的一下用手捂住了嘴。

蓝妹妹扔下帽子。"真正的蓝精灵？说下去，没关系。"

聪聪连忙补救："不！我的意思是说这台机器不适合你这种类型的，呃，蓝精灵。"

"好吧，没关系。我明白了。"蓝妹妹有些沮丧。

健健试图缓解蓝妹妹的情绪。"嘿，别管这个了，我们一起出去玩吧！"

蓝妹妹感觉好了一点。"好吧！"她说，和大家一起玩能让她分散自己的注意力。能出去玩一天很不错，不过他们要玩什么呢？

健健、聪聪和蓝妹妹异口同声喊道："精灵滑板！"

"比萨！"笨笨也同时开口说，"我的意思是……精灵滑板！"

第3章　蓝妹妹被抓走

当聪聪测试他的发明时，邪恶的巫师格格巫也在他那地势陡峭的城堡里研究黑暗魔法。

"就快好了，阿兹猫。"格格巫往他的大锅里倒了一剂药水，而他那坏脾气的老友阿兹猫正忙着用望远镜盯着远处的森林。像往常一样，阿兹猫没有理睬格格巫。

"一小撮蝾螈粪便，一克牦牛脚趾间的钙化真菌，还有一块奶酪！"格格巫从他的长袍里取出一大块奶酪，咬了一口，然后扔进大锅，"应该差不多了。"

大锅开始发出咝咝声，片刻之后，咒语完成了。格格巫用长长的钳子从沸腾的大锅中取出一颗小球，和其他咝咝作响的小球一同放在一个盛鸡蛋的盒里。

格格巫非常高兴。"大功告成！十二个球状石化模块。"他拿起一颗小球，一边不停地转动一边仔细观察。"或者我喜欢称它们为：速冻球！"

这时，一只老鼠在地板上慌乱地跑过。格格巫朝这只老鼠扔去一个速冻球。老鼠被击中后一下子就冻僵了，变得一动也不动，只能在原地惊恐地吱吱叫。

"不用客气，阿兹猫。"格格巫搓了搓手说，"晚餐解

第3章 蓝妹妹被抓走

决了。"

"喵！"阿兹猫拒绝享用这顿"晚餐"。

"忘恩负义的家伙！"格格巫骂了一句，然后决定不理会阿兹猫。"而且，这些速冻球可不是用来抓老鼠的！"格格巫把蓝精灵的手绘画像投影到墙上。"我要用它们抓住那些神出鬼没的蓝精灵！那是我的圣杯……如同彩虹尽头的黄金……"格格巫再次点击他准备好的画像。"蓝精灵的精华是世界上效力最强的魔药原料！下一张。"

下一个图像是数百个蓝精灵、一个加号和一口大锅。

"想象一下一百个蓝精灵加起来的魔力会有多强！"格格巫切换下一张幻灯片。

阿兹猫突然变得非常兴奋。它透过望远镜注意到了什么，并试图引起格格巫的注意："喵，喵，喵！"

"现在不行，阿兹猫！我的演讲正进行到一半呢！"格格巫继续，"我的计划很简单。"他迅速切换一张又一张幻灯片。"找到精灵村，把他们一网打尽，榨干他们的魔力。然后，利用这些魔力成为世界上最强大的巫师！哇哈哈哈哈哈！"

格格巫兴奋地走到屏幕前，屏幕上有头发的格格巫的头正好和他的秃头重合了。

"哦，发型不错！"他夸张地称赞着。

"喵，喵，喵！"阿兹猫激动地叫着，"喵，喵，喵！"

终于，格格巫注意到了。"什么？你为什么没有在一开始就

* 探寻神秘村 *

告诉我?"他冲过去把阿兹猫从凳子上打翻下来。

"喵!"阿兹猫气坏了。

格格巫向外看了一眼,惊讶地发现有四个蓝精灵正爬上远处的山顶。"我的天哪,森林里有蓝精灵!"

由于格格巫不尊重它的功劳,阿兹猫生气地发出低吼声,因为是它最先发现蓝精灵的。

格格巫反驳阿兹猫:"那可是我的望远镜……"。

他大声呼叫正在垃圾桶里翻捡剩饭的秃鹫:"蒙蒂!快来,我的神鹰!"

秃鹫落到格格巫的肩膀上,格格巫用手猛地拍打秃鹫,嘴里痛苦地喊出来:"哦……啊……疼!你的爪子抠进我的肩膀里啦!"蒙蒂稍稍松了松爪子。"啊,这样好多了。"格格巫指向森林,"现在,去吧!去给我抓几个蓝精灵回来!"

格格巫轻轻把蒙蒂推出窗户。那只秃鹫飞走了……

"不,不!你飞错方向了!"格格巫叹了口气,大声朝它喊道。

蒙蒂马上掉头,调整了飞行路线,朝着毫无戒备的蓝精灵飞去。

健健、聪聪、笨笨和蓝妹妹——他们自称这个组合为"蓝精灵小队"——带着各自的精灵滑板,已经爬到了山顶。他们朝下看了看跑道。健健把滑板往跑道上一扔,然后像个职业运动员一

第3章 蓝妹妹被抓走

样跳了上去,他乘着滑板一跃而起,飞上半空,最后稳稳地完美落地。他不禁为自己喝彩:"噢!太棒啦!"

接下来轮到聪聪了。聪聪得意地展示他新型的流线型设计的滑板,不过他在半空中遇到了一些技术麻烦。

"哦,不!"只是聪聪从天上掉下来,落到了健健的怀里,"我猜我应该准备一个降落伞。"

笨笨打算从跑道上滚下来。为了保护自己不受伤,笨笨给自己身上套了一个桶。"轮到我啦!安全第三!"

"噢,天哪!"聪聪和健健同时叫起来,连忙躲到安全的地方。

"哇,哎哟,啊!"笨笨的桶弹出了跑道,把笨笨甩到了空中。"啊……!"笨笨从灌木丛里飞了出来,嗖的一声越过聪聪和健健,猛地撞上了一棵树的树干,砰地摔在地上。

正当聪聪和健健扶起笨笨时,他们抬头看到蓝妹妹用叶子当翅膀从他们头上飞过。

"哇噢,"健健仰慕地看着蓝妹妹在空中舞动,"她真是迷人,不是吗?"

"真是太难以置信了!"蓝妹妹正要降落,一阵风吹了过来。"哇!噢!"她被风吹离了路线,眼看就要遇到麻烦。

"不好!她向禁忌森林飘过去了!"聪聪大叫起来。

"她可不能越过那道围墙!快!"健健领着其他人竭尽全力追赶蓝妹妹。

* 探寻神秘村 *

"哇！噢！"蓝妹妹砰的一声掉到禁忌森林的石头边界旁。

她站了起来，并且有种被监视的怪异感觉。蓝妹妹紧张地看着四周，附近灌木丛中的某样东西引起了她的注意。那是什么？她走近看了看。

突然，蓝妹妹发现那东西也正直勾勾地盯着自己。这个生物虽然躲藏在灌木丛里，但他们还是互相盯着对方看了好一会儿。接着这个生物突然飞快地逃走了。

"不，不，等等！不要走！等等！你是谁？不要害怕！"蓝妹妹跟在后面大声喊道。

当它逃跑时，蓝妹妹发现：这个生物是一个蓝精灵！这怎么可能？

她追赶着这个新出现的蓝精灵来到一堵墙边，而这个蓝精灵穿过墙上的一个小洞进入了禁忌森林。

"嘿！别！你不能进去！"蓝妹妹在后面喊道。她不敢进入森林，慌忙停下。那个蓝精灵不见了，不过他在洞口旁边落下了一顶小小的棕褐色帽子。正当蓝妹妹仔细地研究这顶帽子时，男孩们气喘吁吁地赶到了，他们脸上都挂着担心的表情。

三个男孩都迫不及待地开口喊道：

"蓝妹妹！"

"你没事吧?！"

"出什么事了?！"

蓝妹妹脱口而出："我看到一个蓝精灵！"

第3章　蓝妹妹被抓走

"什么？！"聪聪不相信。

"是谁？"笨笨想知道。

"我不知道，我看不清楚，但他戴着这个！"她举起帽子，正要往下说，突然……

"嘎嘎！"

格格巫的那只巨大的秃鹫出现了，它呼啸而过，抓起蓝妹妹，把她扔进了麻袋里。

"蓝妹妹！蓝色警报！伙计们，快！"健健追了上去。

蓝妹妹在袋子里面愤怒地挣扎，她挥舞拳头，踢着双腿，奋力想要挣脱，但是毫无用处。

健健向蒙蒂飞快地冲去，他抓住了大鸟的羽毛，被带上了天。

笨笨和聪聪朝大鸟扔石头和蓝精灵果，想要击落它。

那只大鸟飞得实在太迅猛有力，就连健健也无法抓住它。砰的一声，健健摔落到了地面上。蓝妹妹被抓走了！

健健、聪聪和笨笨惊慌地看着彼此，这时健健大声喊道："我们一定要救出蓝妹妹！"

三个蓝精灵追赶着蓝妹妹，向着格格巫坐落在悬崖峭壁上的邪恶城堡冲去。

"我有种不……不……不好的预感。"笨笨说道，他的声音直打战。

"哦，是吗？你也认为那只巨型秃鹫会把蓝妹妹带到格格巫的巢穴?！"聪聪挖苦笨笨。

"蓝——妹——妹——！"健健的声音在森林中回荡，他们的朋友眼看就要落入邪恶的巫师手中了。

第4章 格格巫的邪恶计划

在黑暗破败的城堡里,格格巫正和阿兹猫等着蒙蒂。

蒙蒂没有判断好窗户的位置,重重地撞了一下窗台,才从窗户飞进城堡。它松开爪子,把麻袋扔在一个长长的工作台上。

"蒙蒂,我的威猛神鹰,你做到了!你抓住了一个蓝精灵?!"格格巫拿起麻袋,极为得意地把它拖到房间的另一头。

"终于,你带来了我最想要的东西。光膀子的蓝色小不点……"他把袋子里的东西猛地倒进笼子,才发现那个囚犯是蓝妹妹。

"是你!"格格巫大喊。

阿兹猫也发出威胁的嘶嘶声!

"放我出去,你——你这个迷恋蓝精灵的冒牌巫师!"她把刚刚找到的奇怪的蓝精灵帽子藏在背后。

"你就这样对待把你带到这个世界的人吗?我觉得你应该叫我一声'爸爸'!"格格巫把脸贴近笼子。

"我永远不会叫你'爸爸'的!"蓝妹妹抗议。她有一个爸爸,但绝对不是格格巫。

"无所谓!"格格巫转身走开,对着他的鸟说,"干得好,蒙蒂!可惜,这个可恶的生物根本不是一个真正的蓝精灵。"

* 探寻神秘村 *

　　蓝妹妹不小心把蓝精灵的帽子掉到了地上。她连忙捡起来，迅速塞回自己背后。格格巫眯起眼睛，靠近笼子。

　　"什么东西？！你把什么藏起来了？！"他摇晃着笼子，"把它交出来，你这个假蓝精灵！"格格巫伸手穿过笼子栅栏，蓝妹妹努力地躲开了他的粗手指。

　　但她没有注意到阿兹猫在她身后。这只阴险的猫伸出爪子，把帽子抢了过去。

　　"谢了，阿兹猫。"格格巫说。

　　阿兹猫抬起爪子想来个击掌，但格格巫没有搭理它。格格巫对它手中那个奇特的东西更感兴趣。

　　"这是什么东西？"格格巫用放大镜仔细研究着帽子。

　　"喵，喵！"阿兹猫告诉了他。

　　"不同的款式？"言之有理。"是的，呃，当然。我早就看出来了！反正肯定比你早！"

　　"喵。"阿兹猫不满地嘟哝了一声。

　　巫师又回到蓝妹妹面前，决心逼问出真相："你是在哪里找到它的？！"

　　"我才不会告诉你！"蓝妹妹把双臂抱在胸前。

　　"告诉我！"他喊叫起来。

　　"不！"

　　"你最好告诉我！"他用严厉的声音再次威胁蓝妹妹。

　　蓝妹妹的回答还是："不！"

第4章 格格巫的邪恶计划

"好吧，那就不要告诉我！"格格巫想用激将法。

但蓝妹妹没上当："好哇！"

"无所谓啦！我已经拿到了我想要的东西。"格格巫来到橱柜前，开始翻找不同的药水瓶，"我们走，阿兹猫！"

在城堡外，健健、笨笨和聪聪终于爬上了山腰，正透过阿兹猫的猫洞朝里偷看。

健健打出了军事手语，但聪聪和笨笨都看不懂。健健又打了一次手语。

笨笨觉得他已经搞懂了。"哦，我知道了。先向左，再向右，再向后翻个跟头，然后稳稳落地。"

健健摇了摇头，又试了一次。"你是指某个人、某本书还是某部电影？"笨笨低声问。

聪聪明白这个看手势猜谜的游戏没什么用处，他压低声音说："没人能看懂你的手语，健健！"

健健沮丧地说："唉！算了。你俩跟紧我就行了。"

男孩们悄悄地跑过地板，朝关着蓝妹妹的笼子爬去。

格格巫完全沉迷于研究那顶帽子，根本没有注意到健健他们。格格巫扯出一根线，整个帽子都散了。这正是他想要的。格格巫朝这团线挥着手，并开始吟唱。

"万能的虫草和猫毛。"他低声念着咒语，把原料撒在一口大锅里。

阿兹猫看到猫毛愣了一下，再仔细看看，原来是自己的毛。

探寻神秘村

格格巫是什么时候从它身上取下这么一撮毛的？

"告诉我这顶蓝精灵帽子的主人到底是谁！"

所有的成分混合后，产生了巨大的魔法效应。

一个无形的声音从锅中响起："你一直在寻找那些蓝色的精灵，但这顶帽子来自不同的地方。"

格格巫高兴地搓着双手大声叫喊出来："是吗！哪里？！它来自哪里？！"

大锅继续发出声音："蓝精灵村庄，充满魔法的地方……"

这比格格巫想要的答案还要好。"一个村庄？继续！"

"你不要打断我。"大锅责骂格格巫。

"哦，抱歉……请继续。"

"它的位置……"

巫师弯下腰，确保能听清楚位置在哪儿："在……？"

"没人知道。"这是大锅的最终答案。

"不！为什么不早说！一开始你就应该说'我不知道'！你这讨厌的破锅！"格格巫一脚踢在大黑锅上，反而把脚弄伤了。"嗷……吼……吼……吼！"

不过这一脚倒是让大锅再次开口说话了。

"但是有一条线索……"

蓝精灵帽子的线头浮在魔药表面，渐渐形成了一个形状。

"真有意思。这是什么？我懂了。顶着蓬松头发的三根手指的木偶！"格格巫思索着，点点头。

第4章 格格巫的邪恶计划

"喵,喵。"阿兹猫说。这显然是树啊。

"你说这是树?肯定是某种标志或者代号什么的。"格格巫喃喃自语,试图破解代号。

阿兹猫已经走到挂在墙上的地图前。"喵,喵,喵!"阿兹猫冲着地图叫,对着上面一个地方激动地挥动爪子。

格格巫很恼火。"阿兹猫,那不是你的地图。如果你想要你自己的地图,我会给你弄一张!但这是我的地图……"为了让阿兹猫停下,他只好走过去看了看。"等一下。看看我发现了什么。"他用魔杖指着地图。"三棵大树!就在禁忌森林里。"

阿兹猫又翻了个白眼,它干了所有的活,却从来没有被称赞过!

"我们以前从来没有在那里找过。我真是个天才!阿兹猫,看来该出趟远门了!"

阿兹猫不想帮忙,因为它感到沮丧和生气。不过巫师已经开始收拾行李了。

当格格巫因此分心的时候,蓝精灵们正试图尽快撬开关着蓝妹妹的笼子。他们没有太多时间,巫师正在实验室里来回奔走,为"旅行"做着准备。

当格格巫在笼子旁停下来时,他们不得不赶紧躲起来。

"哦,蓝妹妹,多谢你啦!你帮我找到了一群新的蓝精灵!"

这太可怕了!蓝妹妹摇了摇头。

"那些蓝精灵根本不会想到还有我们的存在!"格格巫高兴极

了,"到时候我会……"他装作自己正要偷偷前进并开始攻击。

"他们会全部……"他做了一个惊讶的表情。

"我会……"他举起双手,就像那里发生了一次强烈的爆炸。

"然后他们就会……"他做了一个恐怖的表情。然后,格格巫俯下身,冲着蓝妹妹大笑。

"最后,我将抓住所有蓝精灵,提取他们的魔力,然后变得无比强大!你这个邪恶的小天才,真是有其父必有其女。"他满意地笑了,然后走回到地图前。"好好收拾收拾,伙计们!"格格巫对阿兹猫和蒙蒂说,"我们天亮就出发,吃完早饭,大概八点或八点半……最迟不超过九点!"

格格巫转身继续制定他的阴谋。这给了蓝精灵小队可乘之机,他们终于设法撬开了锁,将蓝妹妹解救出来。

"等等,聪聪……地图!"蓝妹妹用手比画着小声说。

"我来搞定。"聪聪眨了眨眼。他用拍拍虫对着格格巫墙上的地图一连拍了好几张照片。他们以后会用得上的。

格格巫不停地更改他的日程安排。"除去打点行李和出发前上厕所的时间……"

他重新估算了出发时间。"好吧,也许九点半。绝对不能超过十点!"格格巫对自己的安排甚是满意,他回过身想看看他的犯人怎么样了,结果发现笼子空了!

"怎么回事!"格格巫大喊。

在那儿!格格巫发现蓝妹妹和男孩们正跑向窗口。

第4章 格格巫的邪恶计划

"她越狱了!"他大喊,"不!他们知道了我的计划!他们会毁了这一切!"

蓝精灵们必须加快动作。健健指示其他人爬上格格巫的弩弓。

"这东西安全吗?"聪聪问。

"这个弩弓太大了,所以我的答案是'不'!"健健已经就位。

"别让他们跑了!"格格巫喊道。

阿兹猫从房间另一头冲过来,亮出爪子,想要抓住他们。

格格巫也从另一个方向冲了过来。

蓝精灵们被包围了,但是就在他们即将被抓住时,那只曾被石化的老鼠回来复仇了。它将一颗速冻球从架子上推下来,正好击中了格格巫,把他冻僵在半空中。

巫师没法行动了。"抓住他们!抓住那些蓝精灵!"他呼唤他的手下。

"呃,安全带在哪里?!"蓝妹妹回过头,睁大眼睛问健健。

健健告诉她抓紧,然后高喊:"发射!"同时,用力踢开了弩弓的扳机。蓝精灵小队嗖地飞上半空,滑过了大厅,从猫洞冲了出去。

蒙蒂追赶着他们。它从巢穴前方飞出,但没飞多远就撞上了栅栏门。

"抓住那些蓝精灵!"格格巫仍然动弹不得。

阿兹猫快速越过蒙蒂,回头扫了一眼,看见蒙蒂的头被卡在

★ 探寻神秘村 ★

了栅栏门上。

"喵。"阿兹猫说,明显是在嘲笑,"这只笨鸟。"

蓝精灵们迅速穿过了巫师家门口那座年久失修、摇摇欲坠的木桥。

蓝妹妹扭头瞥了一眼身后。"阿兹猫快追上我们了!"

蒙蒂挣脱了出来,也追到蓝精灵们的头顶上方,并朝着木桥高速俯冲下来。

"巨鸟来袭!"笨笨大声警告。

蒙蒂狠狠朝桥上撞过去。由于速度太快,木桥被撞成了两截。蓝精灵们紧紧抓住桥的一头。阿兹猫被吊在了另一头。

"小心!"健健大声警告,断桥像绳索一样朝前方的岩石悬崖荡了过去。

"啊……啊……啊!"笨笨不停地尖叫。

蓝精灵们猛地被甩到山腰上。

"噢!"笨笨没抓住,掉了下去,他的尖叫还在继续:"啊……啊……啊……!"

蓝精灵小队紧张地朝下看着,结果发现他们离地面只有几英寸。笨笨一点事也没有。他只是平躺在下面的一块石头上……仍然在惶恐地尖叫。

聪聪、蓝妹妹和健健跳下来扶起笨笨,慌忙跑起来。

"快!往这边,蓝精灵!"健健带头跑着。

在悬崖的顶端,山谷的另一边,阿兹猫爬上了悬崖边,看着

第4章 格格巫的邪恶计划

逃走的蓝精灵们。

阿兹猫呼叫蒙蒂,指着蓝精灵的方向:"喵!喵!"

蒙蒂飞到空中,越过蓝精灵们的头顶,但蓝精灵们钻进了岩石的缝隙里。

"吼……吼……吼……吼!"蒙蒂发出吓人的尖叫。

"跑快点!!再跑快点!"蓝妹妹大叫。

"为什么我们的腿这么短?!"聪聪边跑边抱怨。

"为什么我们的脚这么大?!"笨笨在第一百万次被绊倒时说。

"为什么我的肌肉这么发达?"健健高呼。

"场合不对吧,兄弟?"聪聪朝健健大喊。

"吼……吼……吼……吼!"蒙蒂咆哮着,再次朝他们扑去。

终于,他们跑到了一截空心的旧木头前,那是通往精灵村的入口。健健、聪聪和蓝妹妹冲了进去,但笨笨被绊倒在隐藏的入口外,挂在木头的边上。蒙蒂直扑向他。

"呃,伙计们!能帮一下忙吗?"笨笨害怕得连声音都发紧。

蒙蒂越来越近了!

笨笨叫得更大声了:"大鸟来了!大鸟来了!"

这时健健飞奔回来,他抓住笨笨,把笨笨扛到肩上,然后跑向安全地带。原木像跷跷板一样抬了起来,蒙蒂飞过了头,结果直接撞在了一块石头上。

"吼……吼……吼……吼。"蒙蒂挣扎着站起来,环视四周。它觉得很奇怪——蓝精灵们都去哪儿了？

蓝精灵们平安到家了，他们高兴极了，欢呼、击掌、拥抱，嘴里喊着："哇哦！""好了！""没事了！"

他们本打算庆祝一整天，但是发现蓝爸爸正交叉双臂在不远处瞪着他们。"你们四个最好给我解释一下。"

他们一下子变喜为忧。"哦，完蛋了。"健健喃喃自语。

"这可不妙。"聪聪说。

笨笨则憨笑着冲蓝爸爸打招呼："嘿。"

第 5 章　蓝精灵小队的秘密行动

蓝精灵小队的成员同时开口，想跟蓝爸爸解释发生了什么事。

四人乱成了一锅粥，蓝爸爸根本没法听清楚谁到底在说什么：

"哦，我的天哪，爸爸，你不会相信的！"

"滑板！"

"来自无名之地的神秘的蓝精灵！"

"他丢了他的帽子！"

"跑进了禁忌森林！"

"可能是另一个精灵村！"

"一只巨大的秃鹫俯冲而下！"

"被锁在笼子里！"

"格格巫有速冻球！"

"他有地图！"

"格格巫会抓住他们的！"

"我们必须到禁忌森林去！"

"三棵大树！"

"我们必须及时赶到！"

"健健救了我们所有人！"

* 探寻神秘村 *

"健健带着我们坐在弩弓上，弹了出来！"

他们你一言我一语，蓝爸爸无法了解整件事情。"一个一个说！停！停！"最后，蓝爸爸吹了一声很响的口哨，才让他们停下来。

蓝爸爸梳理了一下刚刚听到的信息。"我说过很多次了，不准踏入禁忌森林！"他摇摇头，"现在你们却在说什么地图、神秘蓝精灵，还有格格巫的城堡！"

健健看起来像是有话要说，但是蓝爸爸没打算让他们再开口解释。蓝爸爸接着往下说："你们说的这些都没有任何意义！我真不明白为什么你们连简单的规矩也不能遵守。就是因为你们偷偷溜出去才让自己陷入了险境！在我看来，唯一能保证你们不捣蛋的办法就是，把你们关禁闭！"

健健、笨笨和聪聪立马开始抱怨：

"禁闭？！"

"什么？！"

"这不公平！"

"可是，蓝爸爸！"

"拜托！"

蓝爸爸不想听他们的借口。他是认真的。"没有'但是'！除非你们告诉我要去哪里，否则你们一步也不允许踏出屋子。明白了吗？"

蓝妹妹知道蓝爸爸是认真的。他们几个没办法说服蓝爸爸允许他们追赶格格巫。最好的办法是接受惩罚,然后再想办法溜出去。

"您说得对,蓝爸爸。"蓝妹妹说。

蓝爸爸不敢相信自己的蓝耳朵。"嗯?你说什么?"

"嗯?你说什么?"聪聪和其他人也同样纳闷。

蓝妹妹看着男孩们。"您说得对。我们太鲁莽、太冲动了。"

蓝爸爸盯着蓝妹妹看了好一会儿。"呃……没错。就像我说的……你们这样的行为是不负责任的!"

"对!说得没错!的确如此!完全同意。你们也是这么认为的吧,伙计们?"蓝妹妹承担下责任。没有时间可以浪费了。

男孩们都不明白蓝妹妹为什么这样说。他们又开始你一言我一语了。

"是吗?"

"不好意思?"

"呃,你说什么呀,蓝妹妹?"

蓝爸爸恢复了镇定。"很好,那么,还有……"

蓝爸爸准备继续批评他们不负责任的行为,但蓝妹妹打断了他。"事实上,我认为我们应该现在就回房间闭门思过。"

"好吧,我想那是……"

"严厉,但是公正。"蓝妹妹说完,开始招呼她的朋友们出门,又是推又是拉地催促他们一起回屋。"快走吧,伙计们。"

"你这葫芦里卖的什么药啊,蓝妹妹?"聪聪问。

* 探寻神秘村 *

"好吧,好吧,我正走着呢。"笨笨又绊倒了。

"你刚才被鸟把脑袋给啄坏了?"健健问。

"其实,蓝妹妹……"蓝爸爸还有话想说。

蓝妹妹打开门,把男孩们推了进去,转过头对蓝爸爸说:"别担心,爸爸,我们一定会反省我们的错误。因此,我们也绝对不会离开我们的房间,直到真正认识到自己的错误为止。而且,为了防止下次再犯错,我们会多反省几天的。"

"好的,不过……"蓝爸爸摸了摸自己的胡子。

"爸爸,感谢您的教诲。"她最后一个离开,带上了门。

蓝爸爸愣在原地,他被刚才的事情完全搞糊涂了。他回到椅子上,自言自语:"真搞不懂这些孩子在想什么。"

蓝妹妹因为对蓝爸爸说谎而感到不安,但是她从心底里相信,另一个精灵村需要她的帮助。于是,当她回到家时,她开始往包里装出门的必需品:水壶、毛毯、手电、零食和梳子。

出门前,蓝妹妹偷偷看了下镜子。这面镜子倒映着另一面镜子,被倒映的镜子又倒映着这面镜子本身,结果看起来镜子里面有无数个蓝妹妹。蓝妹妹充满自信地点了点头,悄悄地走出了屋子。

蓝妹妹急急忙忙地赶路,她离精灵村越来越远了。蓝妹妹爬上隐秘的山谷,站在高处,最后一次回头看了一眼。如果不找到另一个精灵村并警告那里的村民提防格格巫,她绝不会回来。

肩负着这样的使命,蓝妹妹感到有一点紧张,她一直走到一

第 5 章 蓝精灵小队的秘密行动

堵石头高墙的前面。就是在这里,她发现了奇怪的蓝精灵帽子。她很快找到了之前神秘蓝精灵穿过的小洞。她深吸了一口气,正要钻过去。突然间,蓝妹妹听见灌木丛中传来窸窸窣窣的声音。她停下来,害怕极了。不过她很快就辨认出那个声音是什么,或者说,是谁发出来的。

"健健,"蓝妹妹说,"我知道是你。"

健健走了出来。

"你好,蓝妹妹。"健健说,他身后的灌木丛中传出更响的沙沙声。

"聪聪?"蓝妹妹还没看就喊道。

"你怎么知道是我?"聪聪问。

蓝妹妹笑着说:"还有笨笨……"

嗖的一声,接着砰的一声,笨笨从一棵大树上掉下来,摔在健健身边。

"你们来这里干什么?"蓝妹妹问道,而笨笨正掸掉身上的尘土。

"我们知道你有什么事瞒着我们。"健健告诉她。

"全都是我的错。"她向大家解释道。

"但是,蓝妹妹,你要去禁忌森林吗?"健健走到她身前,挡住了去路,"这太危险了。"

她知道健健是对的,但仍说:"我必须去给那个神秘的精灵村报信。"

★探寻神秘村★

"好吧，我们是蓝精灵小队，必须一起行动……"健健走上前，站到她身旁，"我们和你一起去。"

"你们不必如此。"她不同意。

"不用你说，我们是自愿的。"健健回答。

"我们是自愿的。"笨笨也跟着说。

蓝妹妹很快就明白，她绝对不可能说服他们。无论如何，她的朋友们都会支持她。"谢谢你们。"

"言归正传。"聪聪说道。他把拍拍虫放到一张纸上。所有的蓝精灵都围拢过来，看着拍拍虫画出一张地图。这张地图和他们在格格巫的城堡看到的地图一模一样，上面标记了三棵大树！

笨笨钦佩极了。"哇！虫虫科技。太酷了！"

聪聪研究了地图。"根据地图，我们应该是……"他看了一眼周围，"就在禁忌森林的巨大石墙外。"

他们环顾四周，看着赫然耸立的石墙。

"没错！"聪聪说。

健健正要带头第一个钻过墙上的洞，但蓝妹妹拦住了他。蓝妹妹深吸一口气，第一个钻了过去，她的朋友们紧随其后……

第 6 章　走进禁忌森林

对精灵村里的蓝精灵而言，禁忌森林是一片未知领域。在聪聪看来，他们正在进行开创性的研究！他不想错过任何东西，所以他立即开始用拍拍虫记录下自己的想法。

"四个小蓝精灵的一小步。"他骄傲地宣布……然后撞上了一张蜘蛛网。"哈啊！呸！"

蓝妹妹无法相信她的眼睛。这里的一切都光芒四射、五彩缤纷、如梦如幻！"哇，哇，哇，哇，哇……哇！"她屏气凝神，从石头上跑到灌木丛里，又冲到各种植物前，里里外外查看了个遍。"啊！"

蓝妹妹被一朵巨大的花吞了进去。

健健冲过来，大喊："蓝妹妹！你还好吗，蓝妹妹？"

等健健和聪聪跑到近处，他们也被巨大的花儿吞了进去。

只剩下笨笨了，他慢慢地走近花朵。"花儿乖……花儿乖……"

所有邻近的花儿都朝他弯下身子，包围了他。"花儿一点都不乖！！！"笨笨尖叫着，飞快地转身想要逃走，却没注意面前还有一朵花，直接跑进了它张开的嘴里。

蓝精灵小队被一朵花咀嚼，吐出来，然后再被另一朵花吞下去，仿佛每朵花都在用嘴对他们进行检查。

"啊！啊！啊！"每次花儿张开嘴，都能听到聪聪的尖叫。

终于，花儿们认为自己不喜欢蓝精灵的味道，一个个地把他们吐了出来，扔进禁忌森林的深处。

蓝妹妹、健健和聪聪三个人摔到地上，身上沾满了黏糊糊的植物唾液，但好在还四肢健全。

蓝妹妹看着四周。"笨笨去哪儿了？"

一秒钟后，笨笨被食肉花喷了出来。他从邻近的一棵植物上摘下一片叶子来擦脸。果不其然，他摘的叶子来自一朵拳击花。拳击花开始挥动拳头不停地击打笨笨。笨笨被一拳打中了鼻子，仰了过去，滚下山坡。

"小心陡坡！"聪聪说，但是来不及了。

当蓝精灵小队的其他成员找到笨笨的时候，他正躺在柔软的草地上，闭着眼睛。

"笨笨？你还好吗？"蓝妹妹问。

他睁开眼睛，视线越过蓝妹妹，望着远处天上的一些小光点。他说："我看到了星星。"

他们周围飞舞着巨大的虫子，长着如彩虹一般的翅膀。

"哇！"蓝精灵们一同惊呼起来。这种虫子布满了整个天空。

其中一只俯冲下来。

"看上去很友善。"笨笨向其中最大的一只伸出手。他像和

第6章 走进禁忌森林

婴儿说话一样轻声问:"你叫什么名字?"

虫子嗅了嗅笨笨的帽子,结果打了个喷嚏,从嘴中喷出一团火焰。笨笨的帽尖被火焰烧成了黑色。

其他蓝精灵纷纷凑近虫子,想要看得更清楚。

聪聪很激动。他拿出一本书开始查阅。"太神奇了!一只长着翅膀、能喷火的蜻蜓。让我们来看看……我们应该把它归到哪一类呢?"

拍拍虫发出可爱的吱吱声提醒聪聪。

"呃,也许。应该就是那一类,"他回答,"但我还不能确定。"

"也许是龙……蜻蜓?"蓝妹妹觉得它喷火的样子挺像的。

"好吧,我们就叫它'龙蜻蜓'。"聪聪同意。

笨笨小心翼翼地离远了些。"但愿它更像蜻蜓而不是龙。"

突然,龙蜻蜓抓住笨笨的头把他带上了天!

"不!它不像蜻蜓!它不像蜻蜓!"笨笨看到自己就要被带到龙蜻蜓的巢时大声叫起来。

他的朋友们笑了起来,但是笨笨一点也不觉得好笑。

"呃,伙计们!"龙蜻蜓把笨笨和巢里的蛋放在一起,然后坐到他身上以使他保持温暖。笨笨试图说服龙蜻蜓。"我很好!有人能来帮我一把吗?"

另一边,格格巫、阿兹猫和蒙蒂穿过洞口,也进入了禁忌森林。他们也像蓝精灵小队成员一样,被巨大的花儿一口吞进嘴里，然后吐了出来。

"啊！噢！"格格巫使劲儿拍打着掉落在他头顶的蒙蒂。

"吼……吼……吼……吼。"蒙蒂回应他。

"蒙蒂，快下来！"巫师喊着。他们全都沾满了黏稠的花蜜。"嘿！我讨厌大自然！真恶心！"

其中一朵品尝过蓝精灵味道的花儿发出嘶嘶声，然后一口咬住了格格巫的鼻子。

"啊……啊！！！阿兹猫，快来帮我！不要笑了！一点也不好笑！"

又有一朵花儿抓住了巫师的脚踝。

格格巫生气极了。"该死的禁忌森林……"这下可不太妙。

阿兹猫安全地坐在一旁，笑着发出咕噜声。

蒙蒂也帮不上忙，因为它这时正和某种奇怪的、像眼球一样的植物纠缠在了一起。

"放开我！"格格巫告诉花儿。花儿们照做了，用力地把格格巫吐了出来，重重地把他摔在森林的地上。

蓝精灵小队抬头望向天空，他们头顶有数百只龙蜻蜓飞过，组成了一幅移动的天幕。阳光从它们彩虹色的翅膀里反射出来。树上挂着数百个巢。

"它们的巢是用一种我从没见过的特殊材料建造的。"聪聪看着四周说。

第6章 走进禁忌森林

"哇！哎哟！"笨笨想办法逃出了龙蜻蜓的巢，回到大家身边。"知道吗，我觉得我今天已经受够这些飞来飞去的龙蜻蜓了。"

突然间，他们的头顶掠过一个影子，那显然不是龙蜻蜓。

是蒙蒂，它拦住了蓝精灵们的去路！

蓝精灵们转身就跑，但阿兹猫挡住了他们的退路，舔着嘴唇并发出可怕的叫声："喵！"

最后，阴险的格格巫从巨石后面走过来，面带阴笑。

"嘿！你怎么也在这儿？"笨笨问，巫师的出现让他有点迷糊。

"我觉得在这里安个家也不错，森林里更安静一些。山上风太大了……你们觉得我来这儿干什么，蠢货？"格格巫充满讽刺地吼叫起来。

"你永远不会找到那个精灵村的，格格巫！"蓝妹妹对他说。

格格巫嘲笑蓝妹妹："哦，蓝妹妹！多亏了你，我才知道还有另外一群蓝精灵。抓住他们，伙计们！"

说罢，蒙蒂和阿兹猫朝蓝精灵们冲去。

"分散逃跑战术，快跑！"健健大喊，蓝精灵们应声分头逃散。

阿兹猫和蒙蒂撞到了一起。

笨笨围着格格巫的脚转圈跑，边跑边喊"分散逃跑"。这让巫师纳闷了好一阵,健健则把握住机会用树枝狠狠地击打格格巫的小腿。

"啊!"巫师尖叫起来。

聪聪边躲闪阿兹猫边喊:"分头跑!"

"分头跑!"蓝妹妹朝另一个方向边跑边喊。

格格巫在原地打转。蓝精灵们从各个角度攻击他。他把脑袋往后一仰,不小心把一颗蛋从龙蜻蜓的巢里挤了出来。赶在蛋掉到地上之前,格格巫接住了它。但是上面的龙蜻蜓被激怒了,开始躁动不安,格格巫灵机一动,想到了一个邪恶的点子。

他看着笨笨说:"嘿,小不点!你是那个叫'笨笨'的吧?"

笨笨停了下来,说:"咦?"

"快点想!"格格巫把蛋扔进笨笨的怀里。

"我接到了!"笨笨看了看蛋,又看了看愤怒的龙蜻蜓,"这下糟了……"

现在龙蜻蜓全都把目标集中到了笨笨身上!它们把笨笨和其他蓝精灵包围了起来。

"笨笨!把蛋还给它们!"健健命令。

"好的。"笨笨回答。他想把蛋扔掉,但不管怎么做,蛋最后还是回到他的手中。"哦,不会吧。"他抱怨起来,情况变得越来越危险了。

"笨笨!"健健冲他大喊。

"我还在试呢,"笨笨正说着,一只龙蜻蜓喷出火焰烧到了

第6章 走进禁忌森林

他的屁股,"哎哟!"

"去那边!"蓝妹妹看到前面有兔子洞可以躲藏。他们急忙向兔子洞飞奔过去。

蓝妹妹跳进了一个洞,其余的蓝精灵小队成员紧随其后。

"对不起,我拿了你的蛋!"笨笨把蛋放到地上,立即跳进最近的一个洞里。一只龙蜻蜓猛扑过来一把抓住蛋,其他龙蜻蜓则一起对兔子洞喷火。

格格巫、阿兹猫和蒙蒂开心地笑了。

"哈哈!这下好了,他们死定了。"格格巫兴奋地搓起双手。

"喵,喵。"阿兹猫不太确定,"喵!"

格格巫跟猫争辩:"啊,没关系。损失几个无所谓啦,还有整个村子的蓝精灵等着我呢!"

"喵。"阿兹猫还是不同意。

"噢,阿兹猫,自打我们翻修城堡以来,我还从来没有这么高兴过。"

"喵。"

"行啦,你这个毛球!他们肯定完蛋了!"巫师咬着牙,狠狠说道。

"喵,喵,喵。"阿兹猫在回去的路上继续争辩。

"我说,完蛋了!"格格巫坚持自己的看法。

"喵,喵,喵。"阿兹猫还想说点什么,但格格巫已经不搭理它了。

第7章　掉进兔子窝

在兔子窝里，蓝精灵小队的成员们都没有受伤——好吧，应该说，每个蓝精灵都安然无恙。但这个团队被打散了，蓝精灵们掉进不同的、又黑又深的像管子一样的通道里。他们都孤身一人，拼命寻找着其他人。

聪聪在黑暗中四处摸索寻找出口。

"有人吗？"蓝妹妹喊道。

"蓝妹妹？！"健健回应道。

"回声！回声！回声！"笨笨冲着黑暗大声喊。"我，呃，不是很喜欢待在黑暗中，"笨笨的声音直打战，"我在白天有光的时候就已经够糟了！"

聪聪掌控着局势，他朝着通道大喊："大家坚持住。我们需要找到一条路离开这里。"

"哇！这可真是个好主意，聪聪。"健健哼了一声。他们当然需要找到一条出去的路，但首先他们得找到其他人。

"伙计们……？"蓝妹妹试图和其他人取得联系。

"黑暗！"笨笨说，这一次听上去他更加恐慌了。大家都去哪儿了？

健健试图让他冷静下来。"别害怕，想些快乐的事情。"

第7章　掉进兔子窝

"现在可真不是什么快乐时光。"笨笨反驳健健。

"待在光亮中，笨笨。"蓝妹妹建议。

有一些微弱的光线透过地面的缝隙照射进来。如果笨笨抬头就能看见一点。

"太迟了。"笨笨太害怕了，根本无法冷静下来，"我已经走进黑暗中了。"

"什么？你为什么……为什么？"健健认为他们都应该待在原地不要乱动。

"我真的吓坏了，伙计们！"笨笨的声音很快传来。

"别乱动！"聪聪赶在笨笨没走多远之前大声喊道。他早就为此做过准备了。"大家找到自己的背包，拿出紧急隧道生存工具包。找到标有'照明'的小玻璃瓶，然后摇晃它。"

笨笨在他的包里找到了一个瓶子并轻轻地摇晃，瓶子里的萤火虫发出了亮光。这下，他能够看见隧道里的路了。

聪聪想确认他那紧张兮兮的朋友的情况："笨笨？你怎么样了？"

"嗯……很好，我想。"笨笨说，他借着萤火虫的亮光翻开背包，想看看聪聪在包里还准备了什么东西。

"冷静点，笨笨。我们不知道会被困在这里多久。所以，各位，无论你做什么，千万不要把所有的食物都吃光了！"聪聪想得还真是周全。

"我刚刚已经吃光了所有的食物！"笨笨呜咽起来，吃完的

* 探寻神秘村 *

包装纸也掉到了地上。

"笨笨！"健健翻了个白眼。

"我有压力暴食症！"笨笨已经无法控制自己了。

蓝妹妹喊道："我来了，笨笨！跟着我的声音……"

"等等！"聪聪打断了蓝妹妹，想要阻止她，"这些隧道就像迷宫一样。如果乱走的话我们更会迷失方向。"

"我们总得做点什么啊！"蓝妹妹回答。

"我赞成蓝妹妹——是时候采取行动了！"健健已经准备好了。

"我们不该这样做。"聪聪说，但是他也还没想出更好的主意——暂时还没有。

"蓝妹妹？"笨笨冲着黑暗呼喊着她的名字。

"我离你很近了，笨笨，就快到了！"蓝妹妹告诉他。

"这只是回声给我们造成的错觉而已。"聪聪警告他们。

笨笨还是感到恐慌。"有人吗？！"

"我到了，我到了，就在拐角处。"蓝妹妹走到了一条死路。

"嘿，各位！我的灯灭了。"笨笨的声音颤抖起来。

蓝妹妹感觉到笨笨声音的方向，沿着道路走了过去。"笨笨？！"她的声音在隧道里回荡。

健健听出蓝妹妹很焦急。"够了，我要用拳头为我们打开一条出路！"他开始用拳头狠命地击打墙壁，"哇！哈！哈……哈……哈！"

第 7 章　掉进兔子窝

蓝妹妹头上的隧道开始崩裂了。"隧道要塌啦！"

"健健！别打了，否则我们都要死在这里啦！"聪聪尖叫起来。

"至少我还在努力尝试！"健健继续击打着墙壁。

"我要在这里炸出一个出口。"笨笨在包里找到了一瓶会爆炸的能量饮料。

聪聪连忙大喊："不要啊！"

"好啊！"健健喜欢这个主意。

"不要！"蓝妹妹说。

"太迟了！"笨笨把能量饮料扔向了隧道，紧接着是砰的一声巨响！

"笨……笨？"蓝妹妹找到了他。终于，四个蓝精灵又会合了。

好景不长。黑暗的隧道里冒出无数双亮晶晶的小眼睛，而且每双眼睛都直直地盯着这四个蓝精灵。突然间，地面开始发出隆隆声，一大群绿色的兔子从黑暗中奔涌而出，如潮水般淹没了洞穴。

蓝妹妹跑了起来，然后跳到一只兔子身上，就像跳上了一匹超大号的马。"哇哈哈哈！"

"嘿，蓝妹妹！"她抬头看见笨笨也骑着一只兔子。

蓝妹妹跟着笨笨穿过兔子窝。

聪聪和健健各自抓住了自己的兔子。当健健经过笨笨时，他一把将笨笨抓了过来,两人同骑一只兔子。"哇!哈哈!坚持住,笨笨兄弟!我抓住你了,小伙计。"

蓝精灵们骑在"兔背"上从地下迷宫冲了出来。

一群疯狂的兔子紧随其后,成群结队地从隧道中冲了出来,跑进了森林。

"超速啦!"聪聪尖叫。

笨笨仍然和健健骑着同一只兔子,他感觉有点恶心。"我觉得我要把刚才吃的东西都吐出来了!"

他们旁边的蓝妹妹看起来像个专业骑手。她的兔子用后腿站立起来,发出一种又像兔子又像马的叫声。接着它开始加速,向前快速跃进,并巧妙避开沿途的树木,遥遥领先。

健健和笨笨就没那么轻松了——他们很快从兔子身上颠落,落在了蓝妹妹的兔子背上。聪聪也落在了上面,不过却是脸朝下。聪聪的眼镜落在了他的屁股上,此时聪聪的屁股看上去就像他的脸。

"怎么了?!"聪聪问,他不明白为什么其他人都在笑,"你们在笑什么!"

"这就是我说的'用屁股说话'。"健健笑得眼泪都出来了。

正当聪聪试图重拾尊严时,蓝妹妹发现远处有些东西。"哦,伙伴们!"她高兴地指着远处,"我们现在能看见三棵大树了,大家高兴吗?"

"高兴!"他们欢呼起来。

第7章 掉进兔子窝

蓝妹妹拍了拍兔子的脖子。"快快兔将会以超快的速度带我们赶到那里!"

"快快兔?"笨笨问。

"我觉得它就像一匹马。快看它的牙!"她像骑马一样轻轻踢了兔子一下,"朝着目标冲啊,快快兔!"当快快兔带着他们朝着目标越来越近的时候,蓝妹妹咯咯地笑了起来。

与此同时,在精灵村,蓝爸爸来到蓝妹妹屋外。他敲了敲门,但屋里没人应答。

蓝爸爸隔着门说:"蓝妹妹?你先别说话,请听我说。我觉得昨天可能对你们有点过于严厉了。而且我知道有些时候我有点保护过度。"

屋里还是没人回应,蓝爸爸接着说。

"好吧,不是一点,是非常。但是你们必须明白,你们偷偷溜出去是非常危险的!"蓝爸爸很沮丧,半天没说话,好不容易才平复下来,"蓝妹妹,我知道最近你可能没有意识到,而且我也没跟你说过,其实你……你很耀眼。所以,总而言之,我们和好吧?我想你和你的兄弟们禁足的时间已经够久的了。"蓝爸爸本来期望蓝妹妹会出来,高兴地知道对她的惩罚已经结束了。

结果相反,屋里仍然没有回音。

"蓝妹妹?"蓝爸爸又问,"好吧,我要开门啦,然后再来一场演讲。你在吗?蓝妹妹?"他转动门把手,慢慢走进蓝妹

探寻神秘村

妹的蘑菇屋。很显然,蓝妹妹压根就不在屋里。蓝爸爸感到很吃惊,接着他开始怀疑起来。

蓝爸爸来到健健的蘑菇屋。"健健!"他冲到健健的床前——健健看起来好像睡在被子里。蓝爸爸掀开被子,发现里面是一个杠铃。

"聪聪!"在聪聪的屋里,聪聪看起来好像站在他的黑板前,但实际上那只是一个用他实验室里的物品搭成的假人。

蓝爸爸来到笨笨的蘑菇屋时已经非常生气了。"笨笨!"他掀开笨笨的被子,发现里面是三个苹果。"哦,这也太不像了吧!"蓝爸爸说。那些苹果的造型根本不像一个蓝精灵。

蓝爸爸走出了蘑菇屋,大声宣布:"当我找到那些蓝精灵时,我要罚他们禁闭一个月!"

就在这时,奇奇从窗前走过。"嗯,这里发生了什么事?"蓝爸爸砰地关上了窗户。"嗯,没事,再见。"

第8章　生火、露营、扎筏

蓝精灵小队骑着巨大的兔子——快快兔朝着三棵大树的方向前进,穿过了茂密的树林和广阔的山谷。夜幕降临,月光从树梢上洒落下来。天越来越黑了,快快兔像一个巨大的兔子手电筒一样开始发光。

"哇!"蓝妹妹兴奋地大叫,骑在快快兔背上朝四周望去,整个森林深处都被照亮了,"你们见过这么美丽的景色吗?"

健健转过头看着蓝妹妹,情真意切地说:"每天都能看见,蓝妹妹,每!一!天!"

"别说这种奇怪的话了。"聪聪插嘴进来,翻了翻白眼。

"你才奇怪呢。"健健生气地还嘴。

时间已经很晚了,快快兔逐渐慢了下来,显然它肚子饿了,开始用鼻子四处嗅着寻找食物了。

笨笨已经在快快兔背上睡着了,而且还喃喃自语说梦话呢。聪聪也打了一个哈欠。

"我们可以在这里露营。"聪聪指着一片空地说。他们从快快兔背上下来,每个人都开始伸懒腰。"我来给大家生火。给我捡些柴火来,健健?"

"呃,加个'请'字我会觉得好点。"健健发牢骚。

★ 探寻神秘村 ★

"是的，没错，不过还没有人给我颁发礼貌徽章，所以我才不会说'请'。快去捡柴火吧。"聪聪指着一片茂密的树林说。

健健边咕哝着边捡树枝，而聪聪则翻开书本查看如何生起篝火。

"笨笨，你还好吗？"蓝妹妹坐到他身旁。

"好啊，当然……"笨笨回想着白天的经历，"今天很好玩。呃，没有非常好玩，不过有时候挺刺激的。有那么点。你知道我想说什么。"他终于叹了口气承认。"其实一点都不好玩。"

健健扔了一大堆柴火在聪聪面前。

"干得好，健健，干得好。"聪聪说，他翻了翻说明书，"第一步：柴火应该堆成类似圆锥的形状。"他把柴火堆好。"第二步：用石头敲打打火石，然后……"聪聪试着照做，但除了迸出的一些小火花转瞬变成烟雾之外，没什么效果。聪聪试着冲柴火吹气来引燃火花，但还是没什么用。

"你那不是在吹气，你是在吐口水。"健健对聪聪说。

"嗯，真奇怪。可能是你收集的柴火太潮了，健健。根据手册上写的，应该早就点着了。"聪聪又翻开那页书看了看。

"嘿，我有一个主意。"健健抢过手册，把它扔到那堆柴火上。哗的一声！柴火瞬间点燃，形成了一个巨大的篝火，照亮了四周。

"不，不，不，不，不，不！"聪聪连忙手忙脚乱地把烧得冒烟的书从火堆里抢了出来。

第 8 章 生火、露营、扎筏

"你说得没错,聪明人……你的小手册确实挺有用。"健健微笑着说。

聪聪生气极了。"过分……太过分了。没了这本书,我们会迷路的。"

健健学着聪聪用一种傲慢的语气说:"我是聪聪。我是超级聪明的蓝精灵。"

蓝妹妹正在给快快兔刷毛,被聪聪和健健的争吵逗得笑了起来。他们真的就像兄弟一样,会因为最愚蠢的理由争执起来。

聪聪检查了他的手册。"还好,书只烧坏了一点点,装订仍然完好无损。"他轻轻地吸了一口气,"闻起来真不错。"

蓝精灵围着篝火躺好,凝视着夜空。快快兔吃着胡萝卜和草。

"想想看,伙计们,"蓝妹妹说着,把手枕在头下,"一直以来,我们在村子里工作生活的时候,还有另外一群和我们一样的蓝精灵生活在别处。"

"也许他们和我们一点都不一样,"聪聪说道。

"他说的没错。我们应该做好心理准备,无论我们找到什么,"健健说,"说不定那些精灵甚至都不是蓝色的。"

"也许他们是橙色的,"笨笨说,"我喜欢橙色。"

"他们可能都戴着眼镜呢?"聪聪想象着。

"或者都长着大胡子?"

"他们可能身上长满鳞片、嘴里长满尖牙?"聪聪一想到自己刚说的场景就直发抖。

* 探寻神秘村 *

"还长着巨大的爪子和又大又圆的眼睛。"健健接着说,他的话让聪聪颤抖得更厉害了。

蓝妹妹不相信这些,她坚信那些新的蓝精灵会和她的朋友们一样是最好的。

笨笨想借着火光用手做一个皮影戏木偶。当然,笨笨做得太差劲了,他只把双手投影在一棵树的树干上,"他们也可能有……双手!"

这下,蓝精灵小队的成员都大笑起来。

"听着,他们也可能跟我们完全不一样,但我就和你们不一样啊。蓝爸爸发现了我内心的善良,"蓝妹妹对其他人说,"这些蓝精灵也值得我们去帮助,就像蓝爸爸帮助我一样。我必须这样做。"

"我们会帮你的。我们是蓝精灵小队,我们是一体的。"健健对着蓝妹妹傻傻笑了好久。

聪聪围着其他人走来走去,用一根普通的树枝做成自拍杆,然后拿出拍拍虫放在上面。"来吧,伙计们:蓝精灵自拍时间!"

拍拍虫播放了一段录音:"说'蓝茄子'!"

"蓝茄子!"蓝精灵们一起喊。

照片上的他们都开心地笑着,只有笨笨闭着眼睛。

太阳升起来之前,蓝精灵们又出发了。他们骑在快快兔的背上,经过了一晚上的休息,他们现在体力充沛。快快兔跳过一座小山,突然一下子猛地收住脚,停了下来!

第8章 生火、露营、扎筏

蓝精灵们从快快兔背上爬了下来,想看看是什么东西让快快兔感到惊讶。"从地图上看,前面应该是一条河。"聪聪埋头看着地图说。

"没错。"其他蓝精灵说。这里的确有一条河,但又和其他任何一条河都不一样。河水时涨时落,以一种几乎要把人催眠的节奏上下起伏着。河水清澈见底,可以看到一群群通体发光的鱼游过,还有一些发光的水生物把河水映得晶莹剔透。真是太美了。

健健使劲眨了眨眼。"我简直眼花缭乱了。"

他们爬上快快兔的后背,蓝妹妹说:"好啦,快快兔。让我们看看你能游得多快。驾!"

兔子不愿前进。

"加油,伙计。你能做到。"蓝妹妹鼓励它。

不。快快兔从河边退开,害怕地摇了摇头。

"不过是一条河而已。"健健不明白兔子为什么会这么害怕。

"你想说什么,快快兔?"笨笨好像能听懂兔子的语言一样,"这条河非常危险,在每个弯道都充满了死亡陷阱?"笨笨很肯定这就是兔子的意思。

聪聪不同意。"不,我完全没看出它是这个意思。也许快快兔就是不会游泳。"

健健环顾四周,分析当下的情况。"这太糟糕了。我们本来可以更快地到达目的地。"

聪聪想出了一个好主意。"啊哈!别担心,我勇敢的蓝精灵小队。"他指着他背包上一个徽章说,"我获得这个扎筏荣誉徽章可不是徒有虚名的!"

聪聪参考了他的手册。

拍拍虫画好图纸。

聪聪开始扎木筏。他锯开木头,钉上钉子,不停地忙碌着,直到他兴奋地双拳互击。"看!大功告成!"木筏扎好了,看上去棒极了!

"你真了不起,聪聪!"蓝妹妹高兴地叫起来。

大家开始一拥而上,这时健健拦住笨笨。"给你。"他从附近的一棵植物上摘下一朵像甜甜圈一样的花儿,套在笨笨的脖子上,像给他穿上了一件救生衣。

"噢,既时尚又实用。"笨笨发自心底喜欢这个。

现在他们做好准备了。

他们纷纷同快快兔道别,准备把木筏推到水里。

"让我们把这家伙推进河里!"健健高喊,准备好行动。

"等等!记住,这条奇怪的河里可能会藏着意想不到的危险,"聪聪警告说,"我们一定要小心!"

"要小心。说得好。大家用力……"健健又开始推。

但聪聪还是不放心。"等等!水流非常湍急,我们一定要时刻保持警惕。"

"保持警惕。很好。听我口令,三、二……"

"等等!"聪聪再次打断健健,"我们必须时刻……"

第 8 章 生火、露营、扎筏

"吧啦吧啦梆!"健健胡乱喊着,盖过聪聪的声音。

"密切关注……"

"当当梆!"健健继续。

"水流的速度……"

"呱呱梆当当。"

聪聪只好闭上嘴。

"好啦。"健健知道自己赢了,高兴地笑了,"准备出发!用力推!"

他们把木筏从岸边推到河里,然后跳上去站稳,木筏开始出航。

蓝妹妹向快快兔挥手道别,快快兔在岸边紧张地看着他们。"别担心,我们不会有事的!"

整个小队都向快快兔挥手道别:"再见,快快兔!谢谢!我们回来的时候会来找你的!"

快快兔点了点头,也挥动着爪子向他们道别。

木筏的速度越来越快,笨笨发现了一个控制杆,上面写着"紧急"。"嘿。这是什么东西?"

"最好不要碰那个。"聪聪对笨笨说。

笨笨强忍住没伸手,但他抱怨起来:"完了,我现在更想碰它了。"

"照这个速度,我们肯定能在格格巫之前赶到!"蓝妹妹说。木筏顺着河流飞驰。

* 探寻神秘村 *

　　清晨的阳光营造出一种平静、美丽的气氛。然而，因为太过安静，让人觉得有一丝恐怖。

　　蓝妹妹指着地图说："快看！如果我们沿着这条河流走，我们就能找到……"

　　"就能找到我梦寐以求的宝藏了。"接着说话的居然是格格巫，他说完哈哈大笑了起来。

第 9 章　格格巫的骗局

"格格巫！"突然，蓝妹妹看到了邪恶的巫师，她惊叫起来。

格格巫和他的同伴们用一根漂流的木头做成了一个筏子。阿兹猫正把蒙蒂当作舷外马达，用蒙蒂的鸟尾在水中像水桨一样划动着，产生推动力。

"蓝精灵！"格格巫不敢相信自己的眼睛，"你们居然没有死！"

笨笨紧紧地抿着嘴唇，盯着木筏上的紧急控制杆。此情此景对他而言正是紧急情况……

"追上去！"格格巫向蒙蒂发出指令。

"抓紧了，蓝精灵小队！"健健对其他人说。木筏开始在河水中加速漂流起来。他们把格格巫远远地甩在身后。

"什么……不！"邪恶的巫师从岸边抓起了一根木棍，冲蓝精灵小队叫喊："别再搞破坏了，那可是我的专利！"接着，他急速地向前方划动，追赶蓝精灵，并试着用棍子把他们全都打进湍急的水流中。

健健挥舞着拳头，把格格巫手中的木棍砸得只剩下了一小截，完全失去了武器的作用。

* 探寻神秘村 *

"什么？阿兹猫，给我找一根更大的木棍来。"格格巫把那根小木头扔掉，抬头往前看。忽然，他因为恐惧瞪大了双眼！

蓝精灵小队也被眼前的景象吓坏了。

前方是魔幻激流！汹涌湍急的河水跌宕起伏、波澜诡谲、神秘莫测，处处都是急流和险滩。

"哦，天哪！"格格巫倒吸了一口凉气。他们离魔幻激流越来越近了，阿兹猫紧张地喵喵叫。

"笨笨！拉下控制杆！"聪聪大喊。

"确定吗？！但是你刚才说不要动它！这是个圈套吗？"

"快！拉！"聪聪和蓝妹妹不约而同地命令笨笨。

笨笨用力地扳下紧急控制杆，一根用来撑船帆的桅杆腾地竖了起来。

激流将格格巫和他的木头一会儿抛向空中，一会儿按进水底。

"啊啊啊！"格格巫尖叫连连。

健健操纵着船帆，驭风而行，轻松自如地避开了一个又一个激流。但是又一道大浪朝他们打过来，笨笨被掀出了船舷。

"啊！"他摔到了正在后面疾速追赶的格格巫的木筏上。

格格巫在湍急的河水中不停划桨，他的脑袋在翻腾的水流中忽上忽下。

阿兹猫想朝笨笨猛扑过去，但是一道大浪将它掀翻，也将笨笨安然无恙地抛回了蓝精灵的木筏。此刻，整个蓝精灵小队都被巨浪吞噬了，但是他们仍齐心协力奋勇航行。

第9章　格格巫的骗局

"当心！"聪聪喊起来，他们眼看就要撞上一块巨石。

蓝精灵小队敏捷地躲开了，但是格格巫却没有这么幸运。巫师和他的宠物们没能躲开巨石，他们的木筏被撞翻了。格格巫和他的伙伴们落入了湍急的水流。

"喵。"阿兹猫呜咽着。

"我也爱你。"格格巫对他的爱猫说。这时一个大浪朝他们猛扑过来，瞬间将他们卷入了水底。

"太好了！我们成功了！"蓝精灵们欢呼起来。

"成败在此一举。"

"格格巫完蛋了。"

"再见啦！"

此时他们身后传来求救声，原来是格格巫，他正挣扎着浮出水面。

聪聪没有理会他。"好了！我们没有偏离路线！"他们已经可以眺望到那三棵大树了，它们就在远处。

"加速前进，健健！"眼看快要到达目的地，蓝妹妹兴奋起来。此时她朝后面看了一眼，看见格格巫仍然在急流中拼命挣扎。

"救命！我要沉下去了！求求你们了！我害怕乌龟！"格格巫的胳膊在水中上下扑打着。

"嘿，伙计们，他在搞什么名堂？"笨笨问。

聪聪只想继续前进。"别管那家伙了！"

格格巫继续央求蓝精灵："救命！我的猫不会游泳！"

听见这句话，木筏上的蓝精灵都安静了下来。他们每个人都看着格格巫，考虑接下来该怎么办。健健率先打破了沉默："我们应该帮他。"

"你疯了吗？为什么？！"聪聪问健健。

"因为这是我的行事原则。"健健的回答很干脆。

"听他的！"格格巫趁大口换气的时候说。

"但格格巫是我们的死对头！"聪聪提醒健健。

"格格巫是个不折不扣的坏蛋！"笨笨补充。

"我会做个好人的！"巫师在水中扑腾得更厉害了。

"你们看，我袖子上有颗不折不扣的红心呢！"健健转身给大家看他的心形文身。

"那是你的肩膀，不是袖子。"聪聪翻了个白眼。

"我喜欢你的文身！"格格巫大声对健健说。

健健无法眼睁睁看着巫师淹死。"我们得去救他。"他开始掉转木筏。

"蓝妹妹，劝劝他，让他理智一些！"聪聪向蓝妹妹求助。

健健瞥了一眼蓝妹妹，她沉思了片刻，说："聪聪，我比任何人都要恨格格巫，但我们是蓝精灵，我们要做正确的事。"

"谢天谢地！"格格巫喊了出来。

"我们得救他。"蓝妹妹对其他蓝精灵说。

"我只想郑重声明，我坚决反对这个决定。"聪聪说。

第9章 格格巫的骗局

"不论如何,我们得帮忙。"健健把木筏靠近巫师。

"听起来太了不起了。"格格巫迫不及待地想要得救。

蓝妹妹从笨笨身上抓起一个甜甜圈形状的花朵救生圈递给了健健。"给你,用这个!"

健健操控着木筏驶入恰当的位置,扔出了花朵救生圈。"抓住它。"

"我不知道这样做对不对。"聪聪忧心忡忡地说。

格格巫用救生圈把自己拉了上去。"你不会后悔的。谢谢你,谢谢你,你们真是善良的蓝精灵。"

"你还好吗?"健健问。

"我没事。浑身湿透、筋疲力尽,像个落汤鸡。谢谢关心,但是我还是个坏蛋,所以……"他说着就挥出一拳,把蓝精灵们都打到了水里,霸占了他们的木筏。"好好享受溺水的滋味吧!"他大笑着,"希望你们的水性好过对一个巫师的判断力!"

蒙蒂和阿兹猫舒服地坐在木筏上。

蓝精灵们被湍急的水流冲散了。他们在汹涌狂暴的急流中漂浮了片刻,随即……被冲下了悬崖,坠入巨大的瀑布中。

"啊啊啊啊啊啊啊!"

蓝妹妹、健健、聪聪和笨笨消失在了一片迷蒙的水雾中。

第 10 章　　来到神秘村

蓝妹妹被冲到了一片湛蓝的环礁湖的岸上。她趴在沙滩上，不远处是健健和聪聪。

蓝妹妹一边咳嗽一边急切慌乱地喊："聪聪？！健健？！你们还好吗？"

聪聪哽咽着说："怎么才算'好'呢？"

蓝妹妹四处寻找着笨笨。"笨笨呢？"她问其他蓝精灵。

健健站了起来，掸掉身上的沙子，喊道："笨笨？笨笨！笨笨？"聪聪也加入了搜寻。

三个蓝精灵在海滩上来回走着，呼唤着笨笨的名字。

"呃，这里需要帮助……"一个微弱的声音从远处传来，"我觉得……我没事。"

他们发现笨笨被埋在了沙子里，还被螃蟹袭击了，但幸好安然无恙。不过还是出了点状况。只见聪聪开始搜寻着整个海滩，他情绪失控地喃喃自语："我的背包！我的手册！不！不！不！不！"他疯狂地挖着沙子，气急败坏地把脸转向健健。"这全都怪你！"

"你说什么？！"健健反问，他把手撑在屁股上，随时准备和聪聪打架。

第10章 来到神秘村

"聪聪,别说了!"蓝妹妹站在健健一边。

聪聪迅速把矛头转向了她。"哦,对不起。更正一下:你也摆脱不了干系!"

"别把她扯进来!"健健愤怒地说。

"健健!我不需要你为我出头!"蓝妹妹对他说。

"哦,好极了,所以你现在开始生我的气了?"健健问她。

聪聪指着蓝妹妹生气地说:"你是让我们陷入这场麻烦的罪魁祸首!"

"嘿!我本来是要自己一个人来的。"蓝妹妹反唇相讥,提醒他不要忘了当初她只想只身冒险。

"哦,这下好了,蓝精灵小队解散了!"健健两手一摊。小组成员的关系破裂了。

"我想大喊大叫!"笨笨喊起来,只是想和其他人一样。

"少管闲事,笨笨!"聪聪开始拿他撒气。

"我就是要喊!!"笨笨对聪聪不满,冲他大嚷起来。

健健再也忍受不了。"够了,聪明人!是时候好好教教你什么是礼貌了。"他冲过去要打聪聪。

"住手!"蓝妹妹想阻止他俩,但聪聪已经给了健健一脚。

就在他们大打出手的时候,许多支箭像雨点一般从空中落下。

嗖!嗖!

"快找掩护!"蓝妹妹喊起来。

健健把大家拉到了一起,一个巨大的毛毛虫似的生物忽然从灌木丛里钻了出来，把他们团团围住。

然后毛毛虫解体了，分裂出一个又一个的小东西。每一个都是蒙面的小生物。

笨笨吓得脸朝下，栽倒在了沙滩上。

一个小生物走到他们跟前，眼神里似乎露出了惊讶的目光。其余的小生物用手里的武器戳着蓝精灵们，迫使他们前进。健健抱着笨笨，他们跟着这些劫持者离开了海滩，走进了树林。

蓝精灵小队的所有成员都感到非常恐惧。他们还能回家吗？

突然，小生物们停下了脚步。他们聚拢在蓝精灵们的周围，用困惑和兴奋的语调窃窃私语着。

一个小生物走近他们。空气中充满了危险的味道。

健健走上前，用身体挡住了朋友们，试图保护他们。蓝妹妹越过健健的肩膀向外偷看。

"你们是谁？你们想干什么？"健健问。

"她。"那个生物指着蓝妹妹说。

刹那间，所有的蒙面生物冲过来抓住了蓝妹妹，抚摸她的头发，检查她的裙子。

"蓝妹妹！"健健想把他们推开，但无奈人太多了。

"嘿！"蓝妹妹把他们的手推开。

"看她的头发。"其中一个说。

"还有她的裙子。"另一个说。

"可笑的鞋子。"又一个说。

第 10 章　来到神秘村

"她闻起来很香。"

"她看起来很奇怪。"

小生物们纷纷对蓝妹妹指指点点,评头论足。

这时一个小生物推开众人走上前,和蓝妹妹面对面站着。他们彼此打量了对方一会儿。

那个生物看起来十分眼熟……蓝妹妹屏住了呼吸。"是你!"

对方一把扯下了自己的面罩。

那是一个蓝精灵。一个女孩蓝精灵,和蓝妹妹一样!

"你是个女孩!"蓝妹妹高兴地跳了起来,然后对她的伙伴们说:"她是个女孩!"

另一个生物也摘掉了面罩。所有的生物都一个接一个地摘下了面罩。

"哦!"蓝妹妹看出来她们全都是女孩,"哦哦哦……"

"就是她,"第一个走上前的蓝精灵告诉其他人,"她就是我跟你们提起过的那个蓝精灵。"

蓝精灵们开始议论纷纷:"从墙那边过来的那个?她是真的。"

一个蓝精灵伸出手掐了一下蓝妹妹的胳膊,认真看着她说:"我是蓝丽丽。"

"你好,我是蓝妹妹。"蓝妹妹回答。

另一个蓝精灵揭下面罩朝前跳出来,在差点把蓝妹妹撞倒之前,一把搂住了她。"哦,我的天哪,"她抱歉地说,"我是蓝花花。很高兴见到你！我们没有蓝妹妹，但是我们有……"她深吸了一口气，指着其他蓝精灵说："蓝瓣瓣、蓝三叶、蓝草草、蓝雏菊、蓝冬青、蓝榛榛……"

"嘿。"一群女孩摘掉了面罩，朝她挥手致意。

"哦，还是等一会儿再进行自我介绍吧。"蓝花花对她们摆了摆手，然后转着圈地打量着蓝妹妹。"瞧瞧你！你真是与众不同。抱歉冒犯了，但这是大实话。你知道如何用绳子和树枝生火吗？我知道哦！我可以演示给你看。事实上，蓝风暴能给你演示，她可是这方面的高手。对吧，蓝风暴？"

蓝风暴并不像其他人对蓝妹妹那样热情。她用自己的弓箭瞄准了蓝精灵们。

蓝花花没有让蓝风暴破坏了气氛。"这意思是'没错'！你见过彩虹吗？双彩虹见过吗？倒挂的彩虹呢？你最喜欢的歌是这样的吗？'嘿，嘿，嘿，嘿！嘿，嘿，嘿，嘿，嘿，嘿，嘿！'这是我最爱的歌哦。你的裙子太太太漂亮了！"

蓝妹妹感到受宠若惊。

蓝丽丽想让蓝花花平静下来，说："蓝花花，冷静点，好吗？"

蓝花花因为过度兴奋而呼吸急促，她一边说话一边急促地喘息。

蓝风暴比其他姐妹们更加警惕，她俯身向前，快要贴到蓝妹妹的鼻子尖了。"你们来这儿有何贵干？"

第10章 来到神秘村

"哦,呃,好吧……"突然,一切涌上了蓝妹妹的心头——她这次任务的目的!她必须警告她们,保护她们!"我们是来提醒你们提防格格巫的!"蓝妹妹脱口而出。

"格格……什么?"女孩们不约而同地问道。

"他是个危险的巫师,想抓走所有的蓝精灵以增强他的黑暗魔法!而且他知道你们这个神秘村庄的存在。"

女孩们面面相觑。

"神秘村?"蓝风暴气呼呼地说,"你们才神秘兮兮的,不是我们。"

"我们得带你去见蓝柳柳。"蓝丽丽告诉蓝妹妹。

"我们怎么处理这几团蓝乎乎的东西?"另一个女孩看着健健、笨笨和聪聪问。

蓝丽丽打量了他们一下,说:"嗯……把他们几个带上!"

"来吧,蓝妹妹!"蓝花花有了新朋友,感到非常兴奋,"等一会儿你就会看到精灵果园了。我会给你看我的房间,你可以告诉我格格巫的所有事情,然后我可以给你编辫子。但首先,你想再听一遍我最爱的歌吗?嘿,嘿,嘿,嘿,嘿……"

一个严厉的蓝精灵推了一把男孩们。"好了,走起来!"

笨笨在路上绊了一跤。"哇。女孩子真是爱发号施令。"

蓝精灵们被带到了蓝精灵果园。当他们靠近果园的入口时,鼓号齐鸣。大门打开了,蓝精灵小队发现他们正俯瞰整个果园的中心。他们被一百个女孩蓝精灵们围观着,这些女孩蓝精灵交头

探寻神秘村

接耳，议论纷纷。

"那个女孩是谁？还有那几个东西是什么？"

"哦，真恶心！"

"总的来说，我觉得他们有一点可爱。"

"那些是什么玩意儿？"

"那些奇怪的家伙没有穿上衣。"

"我可以看到他们的尾巴！"

"他们出什么事了吗？"

"他们生病了吗？"

"他们是用来吃的吗？"

蓝风暴把武器对准了男孩们。

蓝妹妹站到了一个箱子上解释道："不，不，不……他们是蓝精灵，和我们一样。不同之处在于，他们是男孩。"

"男孩。"这是一个新词，它迅速被女孩们口口相传，传遍了整个果园。

"男孩，"蓝花花重复着，"这词真好玩。男孩，男孩，男孩，男孩，男孩，男孩。"她模仿着男孩子的样子，压低了嗓子说："看着我，我是个男孩。哈哈哈！"

健健、笨笨和聪聪面面相觑。他们有点担心即将发生的事情。

"男孩？"

"他们从哪儿来的？"

"呃！"

第 10 章 来到神秘村

"太恶心了!"

"男孩般……令人恶心。"

"滑稽的样子。"

"看起来不怎么聪明。"

"他们闻起来有一股土味。"

"一身臭汗。"

"为什么他们的嗓音那么低沉?"

"他们的裤子绑在了鞋上,还是鞋子绑在了裤子上?"

"他们的头发呢?"

"他们的上衣呢?"

"我喜欢他们!"

"我不想喜欢他们,但是我有些迷上他们了。"

一时间,女孩们七嘴八舌地议论着!她们围着男孩们,其中一个女孩戳了戳健健的心形文身。

"聪聪日志——第二天:我们遇到了一种奇怪的新生物。她们有时非常吓人,她们闻起来很香。稍后继续。"

"你好,男孩。"一个女孩说,她伸出手碰了碰聪聪,但是被聪聪一把推开了。

"保持距离!好吧!啊!嘿!别再碰我了!"

"他们是我的朋友。"蓝妹妹向大家介绍,"健健、聪聪和笨笨。"

笨笨招招手说:"我在这儿!"

探寻神秘村

"剑剑、葱葱、奔奔。记住了。"蓝花花根本没记下名字。"我们应该做一些胸牌!"

"等等。你们的……男孩们在哪儿呢?"蓝妹妹四处张望着。整个果园还没有出现一个男孩的身影。

人群中爆发出一阵咯咯的笑声。

"这里没有男孩。"一个声音回荡在广场上。

所有人抬起头,发现一个蒙面的生物站在一个高高的露台上。随着面具被慢慢摘下,出现在大家面前的是一个较为年长、更为睿智的女蓝精灵——很像蓝爸爸。她缓缓地走下由藤蔓做成的旋转楼梯,步态好像一位老妇人。但是她突然从楼梯边一跃而下,抓住一个旋转的花朵直升机,从容自信地落在蓝丽丽的身旁。

"我是蓝柳柳,蓝精灵们的首领。"

蓝妹妹顿时肃然起敬。

蓝柳柳轻轻地推了一下蓝妹妹,说:"这就是自我介绍,接下来轮到你了。"

"呃……我,呃……"蓝妹妹结结巴巴地说。

蓝风暴站在了蓝精灵小队和蓝柳柳中间。"别靠得太近,蓝柳柳,"她警告着,"他们有点不对劲儿。"

蓝妹妹急切地说:"我保证,我们真的是来帮忙的。我们是想告诉你要小心那个邪恶的巫师格格巫。他有一张地图,上面印着一个通往三棵大树的地标。给她们看,聪聪。"

第10章　来到神秘村

"拍拍虫。"聪聪叫道。拍拍虫从聪聪的帽子底下探出头。

出于警惕,蓝风暴拉开了弓,对准拍拍虫。"别想跟我耍花招,臭虫。"

拍拍虫深吸了一口气,从蓝风暴身边走了过去,在土里画下了三棵大树。

"我不想打击你们,但是这些不是树。"蓝柳柳告诉他们。

蓝妹妹和男孩们跟着蓝柳柳走到了一处空旷的地方,远处的景色清晰可见,他们跟随着蓝柳柳的目光俯瞰过去。她指着刚才蓝精灵们到过的环礁湖,在湖的上方……

"瀑布?那些是瀑布!"蓝妹妹回忆着巫师的去处,"那意味着格格巫走错方向了!"

"而且如果他去了那里,"蓝柳柳指着三棵大树说,"那么就会走入致命沼泽!"蓝柳柳对大家现在的安全感到很满意,因此放下心来。"他不可能活下来。"

第11章　格格巫逃离沼泽

在致命沼泽中，格格巫确实陷入了大麻烦。

"救命啊！救命啊！我要死在这儿了！"巫师向风中大喊大叫。

格格巫的头上顶着阿兹猫，手里死命地抓着他的鸟，他正被施了魔法的恶毒的食人鱼攻击着。

在蓝精灵果园里，蓝妹妹告诉蓝风暴："我尊重你的想法，但是你不知道格格巫有多厉害。"她心里明白，即使是遭遇灭顶之灾，格格巫也能狡猾地逃脱，低估他是不对的。

"是吗？但是我并不是不尊敬你，你也不知道我们有多厉害。"蓝风暴对她说。

蓝花花附和："相信我们，他死定了！"

蓝柳柳在一旁建议："蓝风暴，你为什么不去侦查一下，核实一下情况呢？"

"留下你们跟他们四个在一起吗？不可能！你看那个！"蓝风暴眯着眼睛盯着健健看，"他一看就不正常。"

"我们会没事的。"蓝柳柳平静地回答。

蓝风暴叹了口气，随即吹了一个响亮的口哨，喊道："喷火兽！"一只龙蜻蜓从树梢上俯冲下来，降落在她的身旁。

第11章　格格巫逃离沼泽

蓝风暴爬到了喷火兽的背上，问："行了，那个格格巫长什么样子？"

"哦，你知道的，"笨笨回答，"就是那种典型的巫师的样子——穿着黑色的长袍，孤身一人和他的猫和鸟住在一起。说起来挺可怜的，真的。"

蓝风暴很快做了一个决定，她对笨笨点点头说："你跟我一起去。你可以指认他。"

"嘿！喂，喂，喂！"健健试着替笨笨求情，"他不可能……"

但是蓝风暴不等他说完，就一把抓起了笨笨。

"啊！"笨笨的双脚离开了地面，他尖叫着："我觉得有必要提醒你，我的名字叫笨笨。"话音未落，喷火兽已经冲向了云霄。"哇哇哇！"

"笨笨！"健健喊着，眼睁睁地看着他们消失在了地平线的远处。

"别担心，蓝风暴会照顾好他的。"蓝柳柳安慰健健。

蓝花花微笑着说："哦，蓝风暴就是刀子嘴豆腐心。"

他们离开后，蓝柳柳面向女孩们说："好了，姑娘们，与此同时，让我们按照果园的风俗，热情欢迎这些远道而来的客人！"

女孩们兴高采烈地欢呼着，随即向四面八方跑去。她们马上要举办一场欢迎活动！

探寻神秘村

健健、聪聪和蓝妹妹成为欢迎活动的特别嘉宾。

热情欢快的旋律奏响了。五彩的纸屑和缤纷的花瓣漫天飞舞。

女孩们给三个蓝精灵赠送了各种各样的礼物：项链、手镯、小珠子、羽毛、树叶、花冠和华丽的头巾。健健因为这些新礼物和殷勤的关注而感到局促不安，但是聪聪被蓝精灵果园里的奇异风俗和新鲜物品深深吸引了。蓝妹妹完全沉浸其中，尽可能地入乡随俗。她爱果园的一切，享受在这里的每一分钟。

第一阶段的欢迎活动结束了，健健、聪聪和蓝妹妹开始分头领略蓝精灵果园各处不同的魅力。

在一间商店里，聪聪正为女孩们讲解一道很长的数学题，但是他搞不懂为什么她们都在笑他。直到回过头才发现健健正在他身后的黑板上画着一团屁状的气体。

不一会儿，女孩们带健健和聪聪去健身房。健健正努力地举重，想博得女孩们的喝彩。突然，他发现自己的每一次举重都会伴随一声屁响，惹得女孩们哈哈大笑。原来是聪聪和拍拍虫正用放屁坐垫报复他呢！

健健对健身房里刚刚发生的一幕耿耿于怀，他坐在了一群女孩中间，她们正在缝制用来伪装的树叶被子。健健想帮忙缝被子，却不断地被针扎到。他感到很恼火，但还是决定努力做好。几个小时之后，健健的手虽然缠满了绷带，但是他举起了一个做工非常精细的被子，脸上露出了满意的微笑，但好景不长……因为就在这时，聪聪举起了一个做得更大的被子。

第11章　格格巫逃离沼泽

当健健和聪聪去体验新事物的时候，蓝柳柳带蓝妹妹来到了射箭场。蓝妹妹惊讶地发现自己很擅长使用弓箭！在练习射箭之后，蓝妹妹和其他女孩一起去跳花型降落伞。起初她感到有些恐惧，但是一旦掌握了要领，她就能从最高的一棵树上手擎花朵旋转着降落，她感到开心极了。在随后的时光里她们连续体验了太极、篮球，甚至骑乘喷火兽！

一天很快就要结束了，蓝柳柳给蓝妹妹展示了画有女孩们的巨型壁画。蓝妹妹微笑着画上了自己。她的内心沐浴着自由的春风，充满了喜悦和幸福。

蓝妹妹甚至想要永远生活在这里。

在致命沼泽的深处，格格巫仍然挣扎着想逃离沼泽。他抓着蒙蒂的尾巴，命令着："飞起来，蒙蒂！用力向上飞！扇动你有力的翅膀把你的主人带出绝境！"

一条食人鱼咬到了格格巫的屁股。

"哎哟！上帝呀！它们咬我的屁股！哎哟！啊！啊！"格格巫抓住了一条食人鱼，决定好好教训教训它，"该死的鱼！"

阿兹猫注意到蓝精灵们正飞过他们的头顶。"喵！"

格格巫狠狠地把鱼摔在了沼泽里，接着冲阿兹猫嚷道："那个神秘的蓝精灵村庄到底在哪里？！"

"喵！"阿兹猫回答。

格格巫抬起头。"什么？"他看到了蓝风暴和笨笨。"是蓝

* 探寻神秘村 *

精灵！为什么他们就是死不了？！蒙蒂，把他们追回来！"格格巫命令他的鸟。

蒙蒂扇着翅膀去追蓝风暴和笨笨。

因为距离遥远，蓝风暴和笨笨还没有发现蒙蒂。他们仍然在寻找着格格巫。突然，喷火兽做了一个激烈的俯冲，笨笨不由自主地紧紧地抓住了喷火兽。

笨笨依然忙不迭地向蓝风暴讲着巫师的事："哦，他还是存在的。他和他那臭烘烘的猫，还有那只渡渡鸟。他们一路上都害得我们担惊受怕。但是，他从一开始就不喜欢我们。"

"他从来没有找到过我们的村子，"笨笨继续说，"他做了一个计划，想把我们全都抓住。然后格格巫就造出了蓝妹妹。不管怎么说……"

蓝风暴并没有仔细听笨笨的胡言乱语，但是他透露的最后一点消息引起了她的注意。"等等！你说蓝妹妹是格格巫创造出来的？"

"哦，是的。用一团黏土。那个是很酷的故事。"笨笨露出了笑容。

"我就说我不相信她。"蓝风暴皱了皱眉。

"如果你和她变得更加熟悉，你会喜欢她的。她跟你差不多，但更友好一些。"笨笨刚要继续说下去，这时蓝风暴看到蒙蒂正朝他们飞过来。

"等等！有个怪物飞过来。"

第11章　格格巫逃离沼泽

笨笨没有察觉。蓝风暴只好伸手把他的头扭过去，笨笨这才看见蒙蒂正朝他们飞过来。

"那不是什么怪物！那是格格巫的大笨鸟！"笨笨惊慌起来。

"过来，你来飞。"蓝风暴把喷火兽身上的缰绳塞给笨笨。

"呃，那可不是个好主意，"笨笨说，"我不擅长飞行。"

"你以前飞过吗？"蓝风暴问。

"呃，没有……"笨笨承认。

"那你怎么知道你不擅长呢？"还没等笨笨继续反对，蓝风暴就把缰绳塞到了他的手里，自己用弓箭对准蒙蒂射击起来。但蒙蒂很幸运地躲开了。

"他会回来的！"蓝风暴警告着笨笨。

她携带了一批用于射击的弹药，包括蓝精灵果、棍子和石块。但是如果不能很快击中那只鸟，弹药迟早会用光的。"快！"她对笨笨说。

"呃。我该怎么做？"笨笨不明白她的意思。他无意中让喷火兽来了个急转弯，恰好及时躲过了蒙蒂的攻击。

"不错！再来一次！"蓝风暴欢呼。

"好的……"笨笨不确定是否还能做一次，但是他想尝试一下。他用力拉了一下缰绳，成功地让喷火兽旋转着冲进了高空。"嘿！"他感到欢欣鼓舞。

但是蒙蒂依然穷追不舍。

格格巫设法摆脱了沼泽，他站在阴暗的水边仰头盯着笨笨。

* 探寻神秘村 *

"就这样!"突然,他察觉到了一个重要的问题。"等一下!我怎么不认识另外那个蓝精灵!"他倒吸了一口气说,"是个女孩!他们找到了神秘的蓝精灵村庄!"

笨笨驾驭着喷火兽腾挪躲闪,同时把另一根箭交给喷火兽。"嘿!我有个点子!喷火兽,喷火!"

喷火兽用火焰点燃了弓箭的尾部,笨笨把它递回给蓝风暴。

"我喜欢你的想法。"蓝风暴说,她朝蒙蒂引弓射去,烧着了它的翅膀。

"哎哟哟,哎哟哟。"受伤的蒙蒂痛苦地哀号着,从空中坠落。格格巫连忙跑过去想接住它。

"蒙蒂!他们对你做了什么,我的小猎神?"格格巫对喷火兽挥舞着拳头,"蓝……精……灵!!!"

"我无法相信他居然逃出了沼泽!我们必须警告大家!"蓝风暴向家中飞去。

"听到了吗,喷火兽?返回精灵果园。"笨笨说,他急不可耐地想尽快逃离格格巫,越远越好。

健健和聪聪在精灵果园里正享受着温泉浴,他们没有觉察到危险的靠近。健健脸上敷着一张面膜。一只毛毛虫正在用脚为健健进行背部按摩。

"真是……有趣的一天。"聪聪看着他的朋友说。

"是呀。"健健快乐地回答。

第11章　格格巫逃离沼泽

"你是认真的吗?"聪聪说。

"认真的……而且很认真。"健健自吹自擂起来。

这时他们头顶上传来一阵沙沙的声音,蓝妹妹正乘着小雏菊从空中飘落下来。

"嘿,各位!这地方是不是棒极了?!"她神采奕奕,脸上洋溢着幸福的表情,穿着一身精灵果园的传统服装。

她正和蓝花花以及其余几个女孩出来闲逛。

"她是不是看上去美极了?看起来就好像是我们的一员!"蓝花花露出一个大大的微笑,"她应该永远和我们待在一起!"

蓝花花的话让健健感到不痛快。他可不想让蓝妹妹和她们在一起!她是属于精灵村的!

"呃,首先,她一直很美,"他说,然后继续补充,"第二,现在的局面已经有点失控了,你不这么觉得吗?"

蓝妹妹咯咯地笑着说:"对不起,你脸上糊的那个东西让我很难认真听你说话。"

健健一把扯掉头上戴着的嵌着珠子和羽毛的帽子,擦了擦脸。

聪聪也开始慢慢地把自己收拾干净。

健健站起来说:"蓝妹妹,我们已经做了我们应该做的事。这些蓝精灵知道了格格巫的存在,所以来吧,让我们想想回家的事吧。"尽管健健努力克制着自己,但是他的声音里还是流露出了一丝恐慌。他觉得是时候离开了,否则他们会永远失去蓝妹妹。

"回家?可是我……"蓝妹妹张望了一下这个村子和围着她

的姐妹们。一切是那么完美。

"他说得对,蓝妹妹。我们已经出来差不多两天了。蓝爸爸会为我们的离开而感到难过的。"聪聪说,提醒她不要忘了自己属于哪里。

"是时候回去了。"健健又说。

蓝妹妹沉默了很长时间。

"蓝妹妹!"健健希望唤起她的注意。

就在这时,一阵嗖嗖声传来,所有人都抬头望去。

"我们来了!"笨笨在高空中宣告着。他的朋友们惊讶地望着他,"事实证明——我真的很擅长骑喷火兽。"

蓝风暴自如地从喷火兽身上滑下来,径直朝站在蓝柳柳身旁的蓝妹妹走去。

"他们是对的。这个格格巫……他是真的,而且正在来这边的路上。"蓝风暴告诉大家。

"哦,不!看,我告诉过你……"蓝妹妹说,但是很快就被蓝风暴打断了。

"你给我闭嘴,蓝妹妹。照我看来,是你和你的小伙伴们故意把他引过来的。不过当然了,这就是你一直以来的计划,不是吗?"

"蓝风暴,冷静……"笨笨不认同地说。

蓝风暴面对大家,仿佛一个陈述案情的律师。"我们的小金发美人甚至都不是一个真正的蓝精灵。她是格格巫造出来的,这

第11章　格格巫逃离沼泽

是笨笨亲口告诉我的。"

蓝柳柳举起一只手问："蓝妹妹，这是真的吗？"

"我……不是那样的。"蓝妹妹想要辩解。

"她被造出来就是为了帮格格巫找到蓝精灵们！"蓝风暴的眼睛里充满了怒火。

"蓝妹妹是来帮你们的。我们都是。"健健对大家说。

"没关系，健健。这都是我的错。"蓝妹妹伤心地看着大家。她在这儿过得那么开心，可是现在情况变得糟透了。

突然，村里的警报响起了。尖锐刺耳的尖啸声响彻了整个村庄。

"姑娘们！防御模式！"蓝柳柳下达了命令。女孩们迅速返回屋子里，再次出现时已经个个全副武装。

她们昂首挺立，全神贯注，做好了御敌的准备。这时，附近的灌木丛中发出了窸窸窣窣的声响。

"准备！"蓝柳柳对部队发出指令，"准备！"

刹那间，一道夹杂着红、蓝、绿三种颜色的强光从树叶间射了出来。

"发射！"蓝柳柳纵身一跃，攻打入侵者，把他钉在了树上。

第12章　格格巫突袭蓝精灵果园

可是蓝柳柳抓住的是蓝爸爸。他骑着快快兔来到了村子里。

蓝爸爸试图挣脱袭击者。蓝柳柳挥舞着一根手杖，但是蓝爸爸也有很厉害的格斗技能，二人势均力敌，不分上下。他们之间的打斗持续了很长时间，直到蓝柳柳踏入了一片明亮的区域，这时蓝爸爸看出对方竟然也是一个蓝精灵！

他感到很吃惊，一瞬间走了神，这给了蓝柳柳可乘之机，蓝柳柳趁其不备打败了他。

"投降吧，巫师！"她命令蓝爸爸。

"巫……什么？你是……？"蓝爸爸不知道他面对的到底是谁，也搞不清她在说什么。

女孩们慢慢地从树林和岩石后面探出头。蓝爸爸惊呆了。

她们上下打量着这位"入侵者"。

"哦，他是个老头。"一个女孩说。

"瞧瞧他的脸。"另一个靠近他。

"他是不是戴着伪装？"一个女孩伸手去摸他的胡子。

"他看起来可没那么坚不可摧。"蓝风暴说，她开心地大笑起来。

"没错，格格巫！这就是你攻击精灵果园的下场！"蓝花花

第 12 章　格格巫突袭蓝精灵果园

一边喊一边跳起了愉快的胜利舞蹈。

"格格巫？你在说……？"蓝爸爸感到十分困惑。

蓝妹妹从人群中走了出来。"等一下！你们搞错了！"

"蓝妹妹？！"一直很困惑的蓝爸爸看到蓝妹妹后更加迷惑不解了。她怎么会在这里？

"他是蓝爸爸！"蓝妹妹对大伙儿说。

"蓝爸爸？又是一个有趣的词。"蓝花花不停念叨着，"蓝爸爸，蓝爸爸，爸爸，爸爸！"她为自己的发音感到满意，一想到他是个坏蛋，蓝花花举起了手中的棍子，想给蓝爸爸一击。

"蓝花花！住手！"蓝柳柳喊道。

蓝丽丽夺过了蓝花花手里的棍子。

"哦，拜托！让我好好地给他一棍子。"蓝花花感到非常兴奋。

"深吸一口气，离那个蓝爸爸远点。"蓝柳柳对她说。

蓝妹妹站到蓝爸爸身旁，向大家介绍起来："各位，他是蓝爸爸。"

女孩们纷纷聚拢过来，兴奋地交头接耳着，有的拽他的胡子，有的用手指戳他。她们的语速极快，蓝爸爸根本搞不清她们在说什么。

"你好。"

"我是蓝小玉。"

"你多大岁数了？"

探寻神秘村

"你是巫师吗？"

"你脸上的那个东西是什么？"

"它怎么待在上面的？"

蓝爸爸的脑袋晕晕乎乎的，他拨开了人群想让自己清醒一些。"怎么有这么多的……"他把身子靠近蓝妹妹问，"男孩们呢？"

健健、笨笨和聪聪走上前来。他们知道要有大麻烦了。

健健踢着地上的土，避免和蓝爸爸对视。"嘿，爸爸。"

聪聪也不敢抬头。"您来了。"

只有笨笨感到和兴奋，他脱口而出："我骑了喷火兽！"

蓝爸爸对于他们擅自离开精灵村的行为感到很生气，但是他很高兴能再次见到孩子们。"老天爷，谢天谢地，你们都没事。"

然后，他转向了蓝柳柳。当他弄清楚这个世界上还存在其他女性蓝精灵后，他感到无比惊讶。

"您怎么找到我们的？"蓝妹妹问。她离开时没有留下任何线索。

"我，呃，姜还是老的辣，你懂的。"他说。他的话不禁让蓝柳柳大笑起来。

"很明显。"她用戏谑的口吻说。

蓝爸爸没有理会她，继续对蓝精灵们说："听着。你们四个跟我回家，马上。"他指着等在一边的快快兔。

"不要着急，叫'蓝爸爸'的东西。"蓝柳柳挡住了他的路。

"叫'蓝爸爸'的东西？我……你是这儿的负责人吗？"蓝

第 12 章　格格巫突袭蓝精灵果园

爸爸觉得自己受到了冒犯。

"没错。"蓝柳柳回答,"我是蓝柳柳。蓝精灵的首领。"

"这个……恐怕我不能赞同,因为我恰好也是蓝精灵的首领,所以……"

蓝柳柳转了转眼睛说:"随便你怎么说,叫'蓝爸爸'的东西。"

蓝爸爸竭尽全力让自己保持礼貌,但是她简直要把他逼疯了。"不好意思,你可以不那么称呼我吗?"

"不然要怎么叫……"蓝柳柳依然挡在蓝爸爸的面前。两个人怒目相向。

最终,蓝爸爸问她:"对了,你的那些动作是从哪儿学的?"

"事实上,是我自学的。"她说话的时候仍旧盯着蓝爸爸看。

"厉害。"蓝爸爸轻轻点了点头。

"谢谢夸奖。"她回答。

"不客气。"

他们相视而笑,鞠躬致意。在场的蓝精灵们都不明白两人之间到底发生了什么。

蓝妹妹打断了他们:"好了,虽然我不知道现在是什么情况,但是,嗯,格格巫怎么办?"

"这段对话和格格巫有什么关系?"蓝爸爸刚一开口,突然砰的一声。

紧接着一道亮光闪现。

* 探寻神秘村 *

当爆炸产生的绿色烟雾散去后,蓝爸爸和蓝柳柳僵在了那里,一动不动,宛如两个雕像。他们被格格巫的速冻球击中了!

"格格巫!"蓝妹妹惊叫,慌乱地看着四周。他到底藏在了哪儿?

"哦,不好意思,我吓到你了吗?"格格巫窃笑着走进了空地当中,"希望如此。"

他抓起蓝爸爸和蓝柳柳,将他们丢入了麻袋里。

蓝妹妹大喊:"大家快跑!"

格格巫笑得更起劲了,因为他们根本无路可逃。"准备迎接进击的格格巫吧!"他说。

嘭!阿兹猫一个猛扑,重重地落在了果园里,挡住了所有蓝精灵的去路。蒙蒂在上空伏击,它把逃命的蓝精灵们都丢到了阿兹猫跟前。

蓝精灵们陷入了困境。

他们向四面八方逃散,寻找任何可能的掩护。

"现在用长矛!"蓝风暴命令。

几个女孩准备向格格巫投掷长矛,但是这根本吓不到他。"格格巫说了'冻'!"他边喊叫边把冷冻粉抛向攻击他的蓝精灵们。

那些蓝精灵都僵住了,格格巫高兴地拍起手。"这就对了!经过蓝精灵测试、格格巫认证的,A等一级强力速冻球!"

他再次发动了攻击,这一回蓝风暴被冻住了。

第 12 章　格格巫突袭蓝精灵果园

"速冻球！速冻球！速冻球！"格格巫一边扔一边唱着歌。

"喵呜，喵呜，喵呜！"阿兹猫抱怨格格巫唠叨。

"好吧，我觉得就算我不说'速冻球'，它们还是会有用的，"格格巫为自己辩解，"但是我们永远不会知道。"他又朝一群逃跑的蓝精灵扔了一颗。"速冻球！"

蒙蒂帮着格格巫发动空袭，从空中投掷速冻球。

蓝妹妹不顾一切地营救着她的新朋友们。她用身体撞向一个又一个被冻住的蓝精灵，希望能帮助她们打破魔法。

格格巫瞄准了蓝妹妹，但是健健挺身而出，挡在了她的面前。"蓝妹妹小心！"

健健被冻住了。

"健健？！"蓝妹妹试图打破咒语，与此同时，格格巫又把几十个冻僵的蓝精灵扔进了袋子里。

"完……蛋……了……蓝妹妹。"健健挣扎着挤出了这句话。

异常兴奋的格格巫手舞足蹈着，他不停地抓起蓝精灵们塞进袋子里，仿佛往一个罐子里装着软糖豆。

阿兹猫帮他撑起口袋。"喵！"

格格巫对他的鸟说："蒙蒂！把蓝精灵们打包！"

蒙蒂俯冲下来，叼起了袋子。

蓝妹妹是唯一逃过一劫的。她不顾一切地试图把健健、聪聪、笨笨和其他人从咒语中解救出来。

健健用僵硬的嘴唇挤出三个字："你……快……跑！"

话音刚落，格格巫一把抓起了健健和聪聪。

"不！"蓝妹妹尖叫起来。

"这里还有两个！"格格巫把健健和聪聪扔向空中，蒙蒂衔住了他们向黑暗飞去。格格巫大笑起来："哈，哈，哈，哈，哈！"

蓝妹妹悲痛欲绝。

格格巫朝她转过身去。"啊，蓝妹妹，我的小发明！"他柔声地说，"你终于实现了我的初衷了。"

"不，这不是真的。"蓝妹妹哭泣着，不肯相信他的话。

"当然是！不然你为什么会把我引到这里来？你为什么在河边救了我？"他露出了邪恶的笑容，"这些都是计划的一部分，不论你多努力，都无法逃脱宿命。但是现在，你对我来说已经没有利用价值了。"他把手伸进袋子里，说："速冻球。"然后把最后一个速冻球朝蓝妹妹扔了过去。

蓝妹妹被冻住了，绝望无助。

"谢谢你为我做的一切。"格格巫对她说，抓起了最后一个女孩蓝精灵。

蓝花花含着泪，费力地说："蓝妹妹，你怎么能这样对我们？"

格格巫抓住蓝妹妹说："因为这就是她的使命！"说完，转身走开了。

蓝妹妹孤零零地冻僵在原地。

一切都结束了。

第 12 章　格格巫突袭蓝精灵果园

蓝精灵果园一片死寂。

格格巫抓住了所有蓝精灵。

而这都是蓝妹妹的错。

第13章　蓝妹妹营救蓝精灵（1）

当冷冻咒语失效后，蓝妹妹瘫在了地上。她害怕极了。天空下起了雨，她泪如雨下，泣不成声。

格格巫没有冻住聪聪的拍拍虫，但是在打斗中拍拍虫翻了过去，四脚朝天。拍拍虫使劲扭动着，把自己的身体翻了回来，急忙跑去找蓝妹妹。看到痛哭流涕的蓝妹妹，拍拍虫感到很担心。为了让她振作起来，拍拍虫在地上画了一颗心，但是蓝妹妹哭得更厉害了。

喷火兽停靠在不远处。它同样为蓝妹妹感到忧心忡忡。

在黑暗之外的地方，快快兔出现在了空地上。

蓝妹妹抬起泪眼，说："嗯？"

拍拍虫趁此机会想让蓝妹妹高兴起来。它印出了蓝妹妹和男孩们前几天的自拍照，照片上的他们围在篝火旁开心地笑着。

蓝妹妹凝视着照片，越发思念她的朋友们。然后她扭过头。"我很抱歉，伙计们……"她太难过了，无法思考。

拍拍虫用鼻子蹭了蹭蓝妹妹，表示拥抱。喷火兽和快快兔也过来安慰蓝妹妹。快快兔轻轻推了推她，好像在说："你能行的。去救他们吧！"

蓝妹妹叹了口气："不，拍拍虫。我已经搞砸太多事情了。"

第13章 蓝妹妹营救蓝精灵（1）

拍拍虫播放着他们旅途上的录音。一开始是健健的声音："我们是蓝精灵小队，我们是一体的。"

紧接着是蓝妹妹的声音："我们是蓝精灵。我们应该做正确的事。"

蓝妹妹听着录音，思索着一路上的所见所闻和所有发生的一切。

"我甚至不是一个真正的蓝精灵。"她哭了起来。然后，她好像想到什么似的，停止了哭泣。"我不是一个真正的蓝精灵！"

她突然跳了起来，抓起拍拍虫，爬到了快快兔的背上。

他们出发了！

在格格巫巢穴的上空，天空乌云密布，给人一种不祥的感觉。窗外大雨倾盆，电闪雷鸣。

"我们需要更多的能量！"巫师对蒙蒂大喊。

格格巫扳下了一个巨大的精密仪器的控制杆。"快点，蒙蒂，快点！对。"

一块小饼干落到了蒙蒂的嘴里，它正在给机器发电的踏车上跑着。蒙蒂竭尽全力倒腾着自己的小短腿，格格巫检查着机器的各个部分。

"压缩机在急速震动。旋转塔正在旋转。烟雾正在上升。"机器运转了！"起泡器正在冒泡。咕嘟嘟，咕嘟嘟！完美！"

所有的能量流入了一个清澈透明的、玻璃鱼缸样式的离心机里。这些能量很快形成了旋涡，冒出了气泡。

格格巫高兴地观察着玻璃缸。"哦，差不多快成功了。"

蓝精灵们被关在吊在房梁上的笼子里。聪聪试图用手把锁撬开，健健和蓝风暴等待着，希望聪聪能救出他们。

"接下来我们要这么做，"聪聪说，"我撬开这把锁……"

"然后呢？"健健、笨笨和蓝风暴异口同声地问。

"我们荡到那个架子上……"聪聪指着房间另一端的一个架子。

"然后呢？"

"拿起一些重的东西……"

"然后呢？"

"用它杀了那只鸟！"聪聪说完了。

"等一下！你希望我们杀掉那只鸟？！"健健怀疑自己听错了。

"好吧，"聪聪让步，"我们只要把它砸晕了就行。"

这个计划得到了其他蓝精灵的同意后，蓝风暴给蓝柳柳打了几个手势。蓝柳柳对和她关在一起的蓝爸爸说："他们制订了一个逃跑计划。但是需要我们的帮忙。"

"是时候用笼子荡个秋千了。"蓝爸爸说。

蓝柳柳瞥了他一眼。"别这么古怪。"

在房间的另一头，聪聪扭动了几下锁并按了下去。锁打开了！大家手拉手从笼子里跳了出去。健健带着蓝精灵们像表演高

第13章　蓝妹妹营救蓝精灵（1）

空飞人的演员一样荡到了另一个笼子上。蓝爸爸和蓝柳柳紧紧抓住笼子，并用手拽住了荡过来的蓝精灵们。"接住了！"蓝柳柳喊。

阿兹猫注意到了他们，它喵喵叫着希望引起格格巫的注意："喵！喵！！"

格格巫怒视着他的猫，说："住口，阿兹猫！你没完没了的哼唧让我都没法校准我的机器了！"

与此同时，蓝爸爸和蓝柳柳帮助蓝精灵们荡到了旁边的架子上，位于人梯最前面的是健健和笨笨。然而就在这时，格格巫转过了身，发现了逃脱出来、正手拉手吊在空中的蓝精灵们。"天哪！又是一次越狱！阿兹猫！你这个废物。"格格巫一边说一边用网子扑打着蓝精灵们。人梯断了，健健和聪聪被独自留在了架子上。"你们真走运，我的脑袋后面可是长了眼睛的。"

"不，格格巫！不！"蓝爸爸朝着格格巫怒吼。

"安静！会轮到你们的！你们给我进去吧！"格格巫把网子里的蓝精灵们倒进了离心机里，他们旋转起来，身上的颜色被吸走了。

格格巫聚精会神地盯着旋转的离心机，密切地研究着里面的液体，它的颜色变得越来越鲜亮了。一缕蓝色的雾气从离心机里蒸腾而出，随后流入了机器里。格格巫微笑着转动着手柄，突然，随着一阵光芒四射，魔法降临了。

蓝柳柳和蓝爸爸使劲摇晃着笼子的栏杆。"不！"

★ 探寻神秘村 ★

"没错！要的就是这个效果！哈，哈，哈！成功了！我可以感觉到它！我可以感觉到那股魔力！"格格巫利用新的魔力改造了长袍，为自己的巫师造型改头换面。

"哦，吼，吼，吼！"整洁的新袍子出现了。他接着摸了一下自己的脑袋，砰！他的头上生出了浓密的黑发。

"哈，哈，哈！看看我的巫师发型！"格格巫高兴地甩动着自己的长发。

"当我解决掉所有蓝精灵以后，我就会拥有梦寐以求的所有的魔力了！"

正在这时，蓝妹妹从阴影中走了出来。"是'几乎'所有的魔力！"

健健跑到笼子边上。"蓝妹妹！"他喊了出来。

格格巫笑得更欢了。"蓝妹妹？！多么美丽的惊喜。你已经在树林里哭够了吗？"他对准她射出一股强大的能量。

蓝妹妹从窗帘上滑下来。"我已经为这些蓝精灵浪费了太多的眼泪！"

格格巫感兴趣地看着她。"这话什么意思？"

蓝妹妹继续说："我已经受够伪装自己了。我要重新效忠您！我真正的父亲！"

第14章　蓝妹妹营救蓝精灵（2）

蓝爸爸和蓝柳柳从笼子里面望着蓝妹妹。

"她不是认真的吧？"蓝柳柳问蓝爸爸。

"不，不，不，"蓝爸爸向她保证，"她绝对不会那样做的！"

"哦，蓝妹妹，"格格巫说，"我才不上你的当呢——就算我信了你的谎言，你又能给我什么我还没有的东西？一次我感受不到力度的按摩吗？"

蓝妹妹早已想好了答案："要是我帮你找到剩下的蓝精灵呢？"

格格巫大笑起来，好像听到的是一个最好笑的笑话。"对，没错。"然后他想了一下。"等一下，你说什么？"

"只要我告诉了你精灵村的位置，你就能拥有更强大的魔力。"她对格格巫说。

格格巫突然来了兴致。"让我想想，一百多个蓝精灵……那就是十倍的魔力。不，是十六倍……让我想想……"他放弃了计算，"不管怎样！那就是更多的魔力！那你这么做的目的是什么？"

"我已经对做好人感到厌倦了，"蓝妹妹说，"用你的魔法

* 探寻神秘村 *

恢复我邪恶的本性吧。"

"你可以继续为我效忠了。"巫师感到很高兴。

"那么我们成交了?"蓝妹妹问。

笼子里的蓝精灵们倒吸了一口凉气。蓝爸爸悲号起来:"蓝妹妹,不要!"

"闭嘴,你这该死的蓝耗子,我正在思考!好,成交!让我们开始吧!"格格巫开始施展魔法,并把所有魔力朝蓝妹妹发射了过去,"出现吧,邪恶的蓝妹妹!"他向她稳稳地射出了能量光束。

蓝妹妹聚精会神地盯着能量光束,身体开始发出亮光。她周身的光芒仿佛一道屏障,抵御着格格巫的魔法。她竭尽全力地挺立着。

健健和聪聪搞不懂她在做什么,突然聪聪说:"等等!我知道了!"

"等一下!"格格巫察觉到了不对劲的地方,"发生了什么?不!不!你在干什么?!"

"就是这样!"聪聪和健健欢呼着,"加油,蓝妹妹!"

格格巫浓密的头发不见了,他的长袍恢复了原来的样子,城堡开始摇摇欲坠。机器呲呲地冒着火花,因为负荷过重快散架了。

魔法从蓝妹妹身上偏离了,蓝色的液体回流到了刚才被扔进机器里的蓝精灵身上。

第14章 蓝妹妹营救蓝精灵（2）

"不！"格格巫咆哮起来。

蓝精灵们欢呼着庆祝起来。

"阿兹猫！"格格巫对他的猫喊道，"过来帮忙！！给我更多的能量！"阿兹猫跑到机器，打开了龙头，希望补充更多的魔力。

聪聪朝健健转过身。"我们该做什么？"

健健发现了一个勺子，他灵机一动，抓起聪聪的胳膊把他拽了进去。"该滑滑板了！"

健健和聪聪抓着勺子从架子上纵身一跃，一起落到了一把斧头的把手上，随即又跳上了一个木坡道上，最后把自己朝着蒙蒂弹射了过去。他们口中高喊着"蓝精灵小队！"，正好把蒙蒂砸晕在地。随后，俩人落到了地上，滑行了一会儿停了下来。此刻，机器开始喷溅火花，然后因为超负荷运转而停止了运行。

一股强大的魔力形成巨大的旋涡，席卷了整个房间。这股力量越来越大，把格格巫、阿兹猫和蒙蒂统统甩出了天花板！

"不！"格格巫一边飞一边尖叫。

所有的蓝精灵兴高采烈地欢呼着，呼喊着蓝妹妹的名字。他们互相拥抱彼此，跳起了欢快的舞蹈。蓝精灵们得救了！

关在笼子里的蓝精灵们被放了出来。他们爬下了梯子。在大锅里的蓝精灵们苏醒过来，重新恢复了蓝色和魔力。

"我没事！哇！"笨笨说，健健和聪聪把他扶了起来。

"我还以为我们完蛋了呢。"蓝花花一边说一边拥抱着朋友们。

"好，每个人都……谢天谢地。"蓝柳柳感到如释重负。

"我真不敢相信她做到了！"聪聪四处打量着说。

"蓝妹妹呢？"健健发现蓝妹妹不见了。

蓝妹妹在离他们几步远的一个平台上，但是她看起来有些不对劲。当蓝精灵们靠了过来，他们发现格格巫的魔力把蓝妹妹变回了本来的样子——一个蓝精灵泥塑模子。她躺在一堆黏土中，旁边是她和朋友们的自拍合影。

"蓝妹妹？"健健不明白。这是真正的她吗？

蓝爸爸扑通一下跪在了地上，眼里满是泪水。

健健问："发生了什么？"他内心感到一阵撕心裂肺的疼痛。

蓝爸爸解释说："这是她曾经的样子。"

所有的蓝精灵顿时目瞪口呆，伤心不已。

蓝花花放声大哭起来。

聪聪呆呆地站在那里，第一次无法思考。他心里感到一丝寒意。

突然，蓝爸爸跳了起来，开始匆忙翻看格格巫的咒语书。"一定有什么我能做的！"他喃喃自语着，"肯定有个什么咒语或者……在哪儿？在哪页？肯定在这儿……不，不是这个。是哪个咒语？哪个咒语？"

蓝精灵们无助地看着他。他们束手无策。

蓝爸爸焦急地浏览着咒语书，寻找着答案。

第14章 蓝妹妹营救蓝精灵（2）

蓝精灵们泪眼婆娑地看着蓝爸爸，他不顾一切地想要救他的小女儿。

聪聪走上前。"爸爸，"他的声音轻轻的，"这本书里没有我们要找的东西。"

蓝爸爸知道聪聪是对的。他愤怒又沮丧地把书摔在了地上。

健健抱起了变成了泥塑的蓝妹妹。"我们带她回家吧。"

第 15 章　　齐聚精灵村

所有的蓝精灵一起护送蓝妹妹回家。雨后的山林静谧安宁。风呼啸着吹过林梢，点点晚星闪着幽微的光芒。

蓝精灵们围成一个圈，守护着躺在中间的蓝妹妹的泥塑。大家纷纷把鲜花和礼物放在她的周围，包括她和男孩们的合影。

蓝爸爸站在最前面，他说："蓝妹妹从不认为自己是一个真正的蓝精灵，但她确实是我们当中最名副其实的蓝精灵。"

聪聪抬起眼镜擦拭着泪水。拍拍虫爬到他的肩上，也在伤心地哭泣。

健健往泥塑上放了一朵小蓝铃花，强忍住自己的泪水。

笨笨也走到他的兄弟旁边，他拉起健健的手。这时，所有蓝精灵，不论是来自精灵村的，还是来自精灵果园的，都一个接一个地手挽手，围成了一个由两百人组成的圆圈，守候在蓝妹妹的身旁。

风大了起来，月亮从乌云后面慢慢钻出来，发出明亮的光芒。

过了一会儿，蓝精灵们纷纷回到了自己的蘑菇屋。只有健健、聪聪和笨笨还不肯离去。他们手拉手站在一起，闭着双眼，永不分离。

而他们并没有注意到，就在这时，蓝妹妹身上的蓝铃花开始

第15章 齐聚精灵村

闪闪发光。

蓝色的光芒缓慢又平稳地渗入了泥塑中。蓝妹妹复活了。她的鼻翼微微抽动,头发变成了金黄色。最后,她睁开了双眼。

蓝妹妹坐了起来,问:"你们为什么都在哭?"

笨笨依然闭着眼睛答道:"因为蓝妹妹。她变成了黏土。"

蓝妹妹向他走过去。"不,笨笨,是我。我在这儿呢。"

笨笨抬起头,他睁开眼看到了蓝妹妹。他揪了揪她的鼻子,确认她是真的蓝妹妹后,大声喊出来:"蓝妹妹?!你真的是蓝妹妹!"

聪聪和健健在这一刻仍然没有睁眼。

"安静点,笨笨。"聪聪说。

"随他去吧,聪聪。我们都有自己表达悲恸的方式。"健健背过身去说。

"笨笨,你能不能……哦……"聪聪看到了站在面前的蓝妹妹。

她醒了!男孩们都冲到了她的身旁。

他们的欢呼声太大了,以至于其他蓝精灵都跑回来看是怎么一回事。蓝爸爸比任何人都感到惊讶。蓝妹妹大笑着,紧紧地拥抱着他。

"瞧瞧你,你总是能带给我惊喜。"蓝爸爸说。他们久久地拥抱着。

蓝花花弄清状况后,一头扎进了蓝妹妹的怀里。其他蓝精灵也纷纷拥抱蓝妹妹，表达着对她的爱意。

蓝爸爸坐在自己蘑菇屋里舒适的椅子上，他的膝盖上摊着一本书。"嘿……又回到我这里了。这个旅行有点疯狂，不是吗？但是最终，蓝妹妹找到了她存在的意义，并把所有的蓝精灵团结在了一起。"

屋外，两百个蓝精灵正在一起忙碌地工作。

"我们需要两个电焊工带头到上面去！"灵灵喊。蓝妹妹和另一个蓝精灵跳到了房顶上。

笨笨也想帮把手，但是他又跌倒了。"我没事！"

蓝爸爸说："每个蓝精灵都在添砖加瓦。我们齐心协力重建精灵果园，它会比以前的更大、更好。"

蓝柳柳和蓝爸爸依然经常比武，但是现在由蓝精灵们担任裁判。

"从那天起，两个村庄都开始对彼此开放，我很高兴告诉你们，我们经常会互相拜访。"蓝爸爸说。

蓝爸爸开始练习蓝柳柳教给他的武打动作。

"非常好，老当益壮。"蓝柳柳拍了拍他的后背。

"你也不差。"蓝爸爸笑着回答。

蓝妹妹经常在聪聪的实验室里帮忙，也会帮着焙焙在厨房里干活。

蓝爸爸继续讲着故事书。"还有，对于那个最为重要的问

第15章　齐聚精灵村

题——蓝妹妹到底是什么？嗯，这只是一个名字。它并没有给她下一个定义。蓝妹妹可以成为任何人。但不要轻信我的话……"

"蓝妹妹是什么？"聪聪问，"我不需要书就能告诉你她是……"

"滴答滴答滴答。"拍拍虫打断了他。

"是的，拍拍虫，我知道，那正是我要——"

"滴答滴答滴答。"拍拍虫再次打断了他。

"好吧，能不能让我说完……"

"滴答滴答滴答。"

"没错。蓝妹妹是不能用一个词描述清楚的。她太复杂了。"

"虽然她还不知道，但她现在已经是我的闺蜜了！"蓝花花接过话来。

"蓝妹妹大胆无畏。"笨笨也插嘴进来。

"嗯，为什么不把你们知道的先告诉我呢？"奇奇说。

健健把奇奇弹射了出去。"蓝妹妹是一切，并超越一切。"

"她很坚强，"蓝风暴说，"虽然不如我，但足够坚强了。"

兢兢迅速拉下窗帘拒绝回答。

"蓝妹妹是一个真正的首领。"蓝柳柳说。

蓝爸爸微笑着说："她非常耀眼！"

焙焙补充了一句："她的厨艺仍然糟透了！"

蓝妹妹坐在长椅上，看着精灵村里的日常。一切又回归了正常。爵爵在村子的中心演奏着音乐。厌厌走过来坐在她的身旁。

★探寻神秘村★

"嘿!我在这儿发牢骚呢。"蓝妹妹对他皱着眉说。

厌厌非常吃惊,偷偷溜走了。

蓝妹妹大笑起来:"开个玩笑!"

厌厌带着一点疑惑重新坐回了长椅上。他是真的很爱抱怨。"你为什么不离开这儿去别的地方呢?"

蓝妹妹对他露出了一个甜美的微笑。

"或者,呃……我猜……猜你可以坐在这儿。"他结结巴巴地说。

蓝妹妹给了他一个大大的拥抱。"这正是我想要做的!"

蓝妹妹兴高采烈地跑开了。

厌厌看着她的背影,偷偷笑了起来。

所有的蓝精灵聚集到了村子的中心,拍拍虫准备好要为他们照相。

"来吧,大家!到了蓝精灵自拍时间了!"蓝妹妹被她两百个最好的朋友簇拥在中央。

所有蓝精灵微笑着异口同声地喊:

"蓝茄子!"

Chapter 1 Smurfette in Distress

"Many great adventures usually start somewhere interesting. Case in point: This one begins in a secret place hidden deep in the forest. Welcome to Smurf Village, where all the Smurfs live happily in their quaint mushroom houses." Papa Smurf looked up from the book he was holding and turned toward the window, where Smurf Village was bustling with activity. "Oh, what's a Smurf you ask? Well, how about a little background."

Just then, a Smurf came barreling into town, bumping into anything and anyone in his path.

Here was the perfect example. "So this is a Smurf. Tiny, blue, funny hat. And they look pretty darn good in a pair of white tights. What does a Smurf do? Just ask him his name. For instance, his name is Clumsy," Papa said with a knowing grin.

"Hi!" Clumsy waved, not watching where he was going. It was no surprise when he tripped, tumbled, and fell into a hollowed-out log.

"I'm okay!" Clumsy's voice echoed through the village.

With a small chuckle and shake of his head, Papa Smurf went on with his introductions.

* The Lost Village *

"Then there's Jokey Smurf and Gullible Smurf ..."

Jokey Smurf handed Gullible Smurf a gift box. "Present for you!" exclaimed Jokey. Suddenly, the box exploded, and Jokey burst into laughter.

"Just kidding. I meant to give you this one," he said, producing another box.

"Wow, thanks!" Gullible accepted the present happily, but when he opened the box, a boxing glove sprang out and punched him in the face.

Across town, Hefty was doing push-ups.

"Ninety-eight, ninety-nine ... one hundred!" he grunted, kissing his big arm muscles. "And now for the one-fingered push-ups!"

"And over here is Nerdy Smurf," Papa said as a Smurf rode by on a scooter.

"Excuse me?" the Smurf shot back.

"Sorry, Brainy. Just kidding!" Brainy got back on his scooter. "There's also Mime Smurf and Instigator Smurf."

"Watch this," Instigator Smurf said with a mischievous grin. "Hey! Look out!" he called to Mime Smurf.

Mime Smurf suddenly collided with an invisible wall.

"Hmm ... what's going on over there?" Nosey Smurf wondered aloud.

Nosey Smurf was watching everything through binoculars. He

Chapter 1 Smurfette in Distress

checked out Paranoid Smurf, who quickly closed his window blinds.

"There's also Winner Smurf and Loser ... " Papa said, gesturing to two Smurfs playing checkers. Winner Smurf was about to celebrate when Loser Smurf flipped the chessboard over in a fit of rage.

"Karate Smurf." Papa waved to a Smurf who kicked Gullible Smurf in the stomach.

Handy Smurf pounded nails.

Vanity Smurf admired himself in his mirror.

Farmer Smurf plucked radishes from his garden.

Painter Smurf put the finishing touches on his masterpiece.

Baker Smurf set out a cake to cool.

Magician Smurf made the cake disappear.

And there were even more: Scuba Smurf, Policeman Smurf, Therapist Smurf, Table-Eating Smurf ...

Papa Smurf paused at Table-Eating Smurf and admitted, "Yeah, we're not too sure about him either." He shrugged, saying, "And then there's me—Papa Smurf. I rock the red tights." Papa chuckled so hard his belly shook. Then suddenly stopped. "But this story isn't about me. And it isn't about them. It's about her."

Outside, a Smurf with long blond hair, wearing a white dress, passed by Papa's window. "Smurfette," Papa said with a fond smile. "The only girl in our village."

* The Lost Village *

The other Smurfs cheerfully greeted Smurfette as she wandered through town.

"Hey, Laundry Smurf!" Smurfette waved at him, then at the next group of Smurfs she saw. "Hey, guys!"

Papa leaned back in his chair. "But that's not the only thing different about Smurfette," he explained. "She was created by the evil wizard, Gargamel. With the help of dark magic, he made Smurfette from a lump of clay."

High above Smurf Village there was a run-down castle on the side of a rocky mountain. The hovel was isolated, and the weather there was always terrible. The dark sky was filled with lightning blasts and thunderous roars.

Inside the shadowy ruin, the evil wizard had molded blue clay into a small Smurf-form. With a whip of his wand, he used dark magic to bring the clay form to life.

BAM! A moonbeam zapped the clay form, and an evil Smurfette rose from the smoke. This Smurfette was nothing like the one who lived in Smurf Village now. This one had a sinister smile.

Papa Smurf shivered. "At first, she was as bad as him. He sent her to find Smurf Village and help him capture us all."

Evil Smurfette had entered the village with only one goal: She was there to cause trouble.

Chapter 1 Smurfette in Distress

"Luckily, I also know a little magic of my own and was able to find the good in Smurfette and help her to shine," Papa said.

Good Smurfette took a little while to fit in, but once she did, she was everyone's friend.

Papa rested his hand on the storybook that was still sitting on his lap. "But there was still one problem. Smurfette's name doesn't tell us anything about her."

Smurfette had tried chemistry with Brainy, and that hadn't ended well. Brainy ended up falling down a hole! She tried karate, with Karate Smurf as her mentor, but when she kicked him ... Well, let's just say a kick while wearing high heels can really hurt!

"Her name doesn't tell us who she is or what she does. So, what exactly is a Smurfette?"

That was a big question. Everyone wanted to know the answer.

Smurfette tried baking a cake with Baker Smurf, but the cake crumbled. Baker Smurf reported, "Well, she's not a baker, I can tell you that for sure."

Brainy Smurf brought out a guide to Smurfs from his extensive library and started flipping through it. "Hmm, let's see. Smurfette ... Smurfette ... Huh, it's not here."

"You know ... A Smurfette's, uh ... " Handy Smurf didn't have a clue.

⋆ The Lost Village ⋆

Farmer Smurf was equally flummoxed. "Well, golly, that's a tough one."

Mime Smurf only shrugged.

"What's a Smurfette?" Postal Smurf mulled over the answer. "Well, she's, uh, she's ... hmmm."

Hefty Smurf had the answer. He smiled as he said, "She's just the greatest ... "

Vanity Smurf was still staring at himself in the mirror when he added, "The most wondrous creature on Earth! Yes, you are!" He meant himself, not Smurfette. "I'm sorry, what was the question?"

"Smurfette? Um ... Oh! I got it!" Clumsy was one of her best friends. He said, "This is one of those eternal questions that we'll never ever know the answer to!" Unbeknownst to Clumsy, Smurfette had heard them all wondering about her. It made Smurfette sad.

After much thought, Papa reiterated the question, "So, what is a Smurfette?" He shrugged. "No one wanted to know the answer to that question more than Smurfette herself... "

Jazzy Smurf played a sad tune while Smurfette wandered over to a bench and sat down. She sighed as she watched the world go by.

"Eh, what are you doing?" Grouchy Smurf stood by the bench, hovering over her.

"Oh, hey Grouchy. I was just—"

"Leaving," he suggested.

"Uhhhh ... " That wasn't actually her plan.

"This is my bench. I come here at the same time every day and—"

"Ohh, let me guess ... " she interrupted. "You grouch."

"Yeah."

Smurfette moved over so he could sit down next to her.

"I can do that. I can grouch." She tried to use his same voice and tone.

Random Smurf came up to them. "Hey, Grouchy. Hey, Smurfette! Nice day, huh?"

"NO IT'S NOT!" Grouchy was being his best self.

"IT'S GONNA RAAAAAIIINNNNN!!" Smurfette grumped, but it didn't come out sounding right. She wasn't a naturally grouchy person. In her own voice, she added, "Which actually helps the plants grow!" She tried again. "But also means it's gonna be cloudy! So chew on that!" Then, "But then again, there might be a rainbow!" It was so hard to stay grouchy! "But rainbows are dumb!"

Smurfette shook her head. She just couldn't do it. "Just kidding, I love rainbows! GAHHH!!"

"You're not very good at this, are you?" Grouchy Smurf asked with a grouchy sigh.

"Uh, no I'm not," she admitted.

• The Lost Village •

"In fact, you're actually kinda bad at it." Grouchy Smurf was still the only grouch in town.

"Yup." Smurfette started to leave, but then she stopped and turned back.

"But you're also bad at it!" Oh that was awful. "That's a lie! You're really, really good at it!"

In the end, only one thing was certain: Smurfette still didn't know what it meant to be a Smurfette!

Chapter 2 Smurfy Thing Finder

Smurfette went to Brainy's mushroom. She was about to knock on the door when Brainy Smurf popped out. He was wearing a lab coat, looking frazzled.

"Hi, Brainy!" Smurfette was happy to see him.

Brainy coughed. "Ahh, Smurfette! Thank goodness you're here!" He leaned past her, glanced around nervously, and grabbed her arm, dragging her inside.

Smurfette began to protest. "I was just—Whoa!" In Brainy's lab, Hefty Smurf was sitting in a chair. On his head was a ridiculous hat made from an old spaghetti colander and some root vegetables. It was connected by wires to a machine that rattled and hummed.

"We're running trials on my new invention, the Smurfy Thing Finder. Test subject: Hefty Smurf," Brainy explained to her.

"Hey, Smurfette." Hefty waved.

"Uh ... hey. That thing's safe right?" Smurfette whispered to Brainy. She became even more worried when she saw Brainy duck behind a blast shield for protection.

"Is it safe?" Brainy brushed her worry away. "Psshh. Of course." He

★ The Lost Village ★

paused, took a deep breath, and warned her, "I'd get back here if I were you."

Smurfette considered what to do, then decided to join Brainy behind the blast shield, leaving Hefty on his own. Brainy recorded the experiment with his "Snappy Bug." It was the Smurf equivalent to a smartphone, but it was also an actual ladybug.

"Snappy Bug, take this down. Smurfy Thing Finder, Trial 1.03." He looked up and asked, "Ready, Hefty?"

"Roger that!" Hefty gave a thumbs-up.

The contraption powered up, set to full throttle. There were a series of scientific beeps and whistles while a string of lights glowed between the helmet and a prognosis dial. The dial spun wildly before stopping on an icon. It was a picture of a big arm muscle.

"Whoa!" Smurfette gasped.

"Ha-ha! It works!" Brainy cheered.

Snappy Bug celebrated too.

"Wow! This thing really gets me," Hefty said, flexing his arm.

Brainy told Smurfette, "It's able to hone in on Hefty's dominant trait—"

"Superstrength!" Hefty said joyfully, kissing his bicep.

"Which I distill into this," Brainy held up a drink can. "I call it Brainy's Super Smurfy Power Fuel." He passed the can to Smurfette.

Chapter 2 Smurfy Thing Finder

"Here. You can try it first!"

Smurfette examined the drink, uncertain if she should try it.

Rushing away from her and the can, Brainy leaped behind the protective blast shield. "All clear!" he shouted, meaning she should drink up.

Smurfette shook her head. "Yeah, see, when you say things like 'all clear', it make me not want to drink it."

The mushroom door flung open as Clumsy burst into the room.

"Hey, guys!" He knocked the drink right out of Smurfette's hand and BOOM! It exploded, leaving a gaping and smoking hole in the wall.

Whew! Smurfette was glad she didn't drink it!

"Hi, Clumsy," they all said together.

"You're just in time to witness scientific history," Brainy began. Looking up, he noticed that through the hole left by the blast, Nosey Smurf was casually strolling by, slowing taking in what had happened.

"What's going on in here?" Nosey said, nosing around.

Brainy, Hefty, Smurfette, and Clumsy all told him, "None of your business, Nosey!"

"Hmmm, well, all right." Nosey wasn't offended. He simply continued on his way.

Suddenly, Smurfette had an idea! Maybe now she could finally learn what her name meant! "Hey! If that vegetable hat can tell us that Hefty

⋆ The Lost Village ⋆

is strong, maybe it can tell me what an 'ette' is." She rushed forward and put on the odd helmet. "Power it up, Brainy!"

The boys gathered behind the blast shield as Brainy powered up the machine.

Brainy flipped a switch, and another series of scientific beeps, whistles, and lights went off until the machine started to spark and smoke. It was shaking. The whole mushroom house rumbled. Candles blew out. All of Brainy's furniture was magnetically pulled toward Smurfette until finally the contraption sputtered to a stop, causing the vegetables on the helmet to wither and wilt.

"Whoa!" Brainy exclaimed, coming out from behind the barrier. "Fascinating!"

"What happened?!" Smurfette was baffled. Why didn't it work like it did for Hefty?

"Somehow, instead of sending energy out, you absorbed it. Probably something to do with the fact that you're not a real—" Slamming a hand over his mouth, Brainy stopped talking.

Smurfette threw down the helmet. "A real Smurf? Go ahead, you can say it."

Brainy immediately said, "No! I just meant this machine wasn't built for a Smurf of your, well, origins."

"Yeah, it's okay. I get it." Smurfette was upset.

Hefty tried to lighten the mood. "Hey, you know what? Let's all go have some fun!"

That made Smurfette feel a little better. "Yeah!" she said, allowing them to distract her. It would be nice to have a day out. But what should they do?

Hefty, Brainy, and Smurfette all agreed. "Smurfboarding!"

"Pizza!" Clumsy said at the same time. "I mean smurfboarding!"

Chapter 3 Smurfette was Captured

While Brainy was trying out his invention, the evil wizard Gargamel was in his craggy hovel, working on his own creation.

"It's almost ready, Azrael." Gargamel mixed a potion in his cauldron while his nasty sidekick cat was busy looking out at the forest through a telescope. He ignored Gargamel—like usual.

"A pinch of newt poo, a gram of calcified fungus from between the toes of a yak, and a piece of cheese!" Gargamel took the chunk of cheese from his robe and ate a bite before adding it to the cauldron. "That oughta do it."

The cauldron began to sizzle, and a moment later, the spell was complete. Using long tongs, he removed an orb from the boiling cauldron and placed it in an egg carton with other sizzling orbs.

Gargamel was pleased. "Presto! Twelve spherical petrification modules." He rotated one for a better look. "Or as I like to call 'em: Freeze Balls!"

Just for fun, Gargamel tossed one at a mouse that was scurrying across the floor. It struck the rodent, which became frozen and motionless. It squeaked in horror.

Chapter 3 Smurfette was Captured

"You're welcome, Azrael." Gargamel rubbed his hands together. "Dinner is served."

"Meow!" Azrael rejected the gift.

"Ingrate!" the wizard spat, then decided he didn't care what the cat thought. "Besides, these Freeze Balls aren't for catching mice!" Gargamel projected hand-drawn images of Smurfs up onto the wall. "They're for capturing those elusive Smurfs! My holy grail ... The gold at the end of my rainbow ... " Gargamel clicked through a presentation he'd prepared. "Their essence is the most potent, magical ingredient in the world! Next slide."

The next image was of hundreds of Smurfs, a plus sign, and a cauldron.

"Imagine the power in a hundred of them combined!" Gargamel went to the next slide.

Azrael suddenly got very excited. He noticed something through the telescope and tried to get Gargamel's attention. "Meow, meow, MEOW!"

"Not now, Azrael! I'm in a middle of a lecture!" The wizard went on saying, "My plan is simple." He rapidly flipped through slide after slide. "Find Smurf Village. Capture all the Smurfs. Drain them of their magic. And finally, use that magic to become the most powerful wizard in the world! Mwahahahaha!"

Gargamel stepped in front of the screen, the on-screen image of

⋆ The Lost Village ⋆

himself with hair shone over his own bald head.

"Ooooh, look at me with hair!" he gushed.

"Meow, meow, MEOW!" Azrael was frantic. "Meow, meow, MEOW!"

Finally, Gargamel took notice. "What? Why didn't you say so in the first place?" He dashed over and knocked Azrael off the stool.

"MEOW!" Azrael complained.

Gargamel peered out and was surprised to see four Smurfs climbing to the top of a hill in the distance. "Blue blazes, I've spotted Smurfs in the forest!"

Azrael growled, offended by the lack of respect, since he was the one who had seen them first.

The wizard growled back. "Well, it's MY telescope ... "

He called to his vulture who was at the garbage can picking through leftover scraps. "Monty! Come, my majestic eagle!"

The vulture landed on Gargamel's shoulder, causing him to cry out in pain while swatting at the bird. "Oooh—Ahh—Ouch. Your talons are digging into my shoulders!" Monty loosened his grip slightly. "Yes, that's better." Gargamel pointed at the forest. "Now, fly! Go capture me some Smurfs!"

Gargamel gave Monty a small push out the window. The bird took off—

Chapter 3 Smurfette was Captured

"No, no! You're going the wrong way!" Gargamel called with a sigh.

Turning back, Monty adjusted his flight path and headed off toward the unsuspecting Smurfs.

Hefty, Brainy, Clumsy, and Smurfette—or "Team Smurf" as they called themselves—arrived at the mountaintop, holding their smurfboards. They looked down at the course below. Hefty tossed his board over the edge and jumped onto it like a pro. "Whoa!! Yeah!!" he cheered as he soared through the air and stuck an awesome landing.

It was Brainy's turn next. He showed off his new streamlined smurfboard, but he had some technical difficulties midair.

"Oh no!" Brainy exclaimed as he fell out of the sky and landed in Hefty's arms. "I guess I should've packed a parachute."

Clumsy was ready to roll. He harnessed himself into a barrel for protection on all sides. "My turn! Safety third!"

"Oh boy," Brainy and Hefty said at the same time, ducking for cover.

"Whoa, whoa, whoa!" The barrel bounced off course and sent Clumsy flying. "AHHHHHHH!" Crashing out of a bush, zooming past Brainy and Hefty, Clumsy ran smack into a tree trunk and landed with a thud!

⋆ The Lost Village ⋆

While the others helped Clumsy, they looked up to see Smurfette flying above them, using leaves as wings.

"Wow," Hefty said, admiring how she soared. "Really takes your breath away, doesn't she?"

"This is incredible!" Smurfette was about to land when a gust of wind caught her leaf-wings. "Whoa! Uh-oh!" She was being blown off course, heading for trouble.

"Oh no! She's getting way too close to the Forbidden Forest!" Brainy shouted.

"She can't go over that wall! Come on!" Hefty led the others. They ran as fast as they could after her.

"Whoooooaa! Oof!" Smurfette landed with a thud on the ground by the big stone boundary to the Forbidden Forest.

She stood, but she had the eerie feeling she was being watched. Glancing around nervously, something caught her eye in a nearby bush. What was it? She looked closer.

Suddenly, there were eyes staring right back at her. The creature was camouflaged by the bush, but they each stared into the other's eyes for a long beat before the creature took off running.

"No, no, no, wait! Don't go! Wait, wait! Who are you? Don't be afraid!" Smurfette called after it.

As it fled, Smurfette noticed something: The creature was a Smurf!

Chapter 3 Smurfette was Captured

How was that possible?!

She chased the new Smurf all the way to a wall, where he dashed through a small hole into the Forbidden Forest.

"Hey! No! You can't go in there!" Smurfette called after him. She didn't dare enter the forest and skidded to a stop. The Smurf disappeared, but beside the hole, there was a tiny tan hat he had left behind. Smurfette was studying it when the boys arrived, out of breath and worried.

They all talked at once:

"Smurfette!"

"You okay?!"

"What happened?!"

Smurfette blurted out, "I saw a Smurf!"

"What?!" Brainy didn't believe her.

"Who was it?" Clumsy wanted to know.

"I don't know, I couldn't get a good look, but he was wearing this!" She held up the hat. She was about to say more, when suddenly—

"Ca-CAW!"

Gargamel's huge bird appeared, and with a might whoosh, he snatched Smurfette up and tossed her into a burlap sack.

"Smurfette! Code blue! Guys, c'mon!" Hefty gave chase.

Inside the sack, Smurfette put up an angry fight, fists flying, legs kicking, struggling to break free, but it was no use.

* The Lost Village *

Hefty ran fast and lunged for Monty, getting a hold of his feathers right before he lifted off.

Clumsy and Brainy launched rocks and Smurfberries at the bird, trying to knock him down.

The bird flew strong, and even Hefty was unable to hold on. With a thud, he fell to the ground. And Smurfette was carried away!

Hefty, Brainy, and Clumsy exchanged terrified looks as Hefty announced, "We gotta get her!"

The Smurfs sprinted after Smurfette as she was carried toward Gargamel's wretched cliffside hovel.

"I have a baaaad feeling about this," Clumsy said, his voice shaking.

"Oh, do you? Does it have to do with the giant vulture carrying our friend off to Gargamel's lair?!" Brainy asked sarcastically.

"Smurfeeeeeetttttteeee!" Hefty's voice echoed through the forest while their friend was delivered to the evil wizard.

Chapter 4 Gargamel's Evil Plan

Inside Gargamel's dark, ruined castle, the wizard and his cat awaited Monty's return.

Monty misjudged the opening and hit the windowsill with a tremendous crash before finding his way inside. Opening his talons, he dropped the burlap sack on a long worktable.

"Monty, my regal raptor, you've done it! You caught a Smurf?!" Gargamel picked up the sack and paraded it across the room.

"Finally, you bring me what I've been asking for. A tiny, blue-skinned, shirtless—" He shoved the contents of the bag into a cage, only to realize the prisoner was Smurfette.

"YOU!" Gargamel shouted at her.

Azrael hissed!

"Let me outta here you—you Smurf-obsessed wannabe wizard!" She hid the strange Smurf hat that she'd found behind her back.

"Is that any way to treat the man who brought you into this world? I'd prefer it if you just called me Papa!" Gargamel put his face close to the cage.

"I would never call you that!" Smurfette protested. She had a papa,

★ The Lost Village ★

and it certainly wasn't Gargamel.

"Your loss!" He moved away. Then, turning to his bird, he said, "Nice catch, Monty! Unfortunately, this vile creature isn't even a real Smurf."

Smurfette accidentally dropped the Smurf hat. She snatched it up and then quickly shoved it behind her back again. Gargamel narrowed his eyes and leaned in.

"What's this?! What are you hiding?!" He shook the cage. "Hand it over you pseudo-Smurf!" Gargamel reached through the bars, but Smurfette dodged his thick fingers.

She didn't notice that Azrael was behind her. The mangy cat managed to nip the hat away from her.

"Thank you, Azrael," Gargamel said.

Azrael put up his paw for a high five, but Gargamel left him hanging. He was more interested in the odd object he was holding.

"What do have we here? Hmmm." Gargamel studied the hat under a magnifying glass.

"Meow. Meow," Azrael told him.

"A different design?" That made sense. "Yes, uh, of course. I noticed that right away! Slightly before you did, in fact!"

"Meow," Azrael grunted.

The wizard crossed back to Smurfette, determined to get the truth. "Where did you get it?!"

Chapter 4 Gargamel's Evil Plan

"I'm not telling you anything!" She crossed her arms over her chest.

"TELL ME!" he shouted.

"NO!"

"You better tell me!" he tried again in a stern voice.

Smurfette's answer was the same. "NO!"

"Fine, don't tell me!" Gargamel said, trying some reverse psychology ...

But that didn't work on Smurfette. "I won't!"

"Who cares! You've already given me what I needed." Gargamel went to his cabinet and began rummaging through different potion bottles. "Come along, Azrael!"

Outside, Hefty, Clumsy, and Brainy had finally made their way up the mountainside and were peeking in through Azrael's cat door.

Hefty made military hand signals, but Brainy and Clumsy didn't understand them. He tried again.

Clumsy thought he had it all figured out. "Oh, I know this. Go left, then right, back handspring, stick the landing."

Hefty shook his head and tried again. "Is it a person, book, or movie?" Clumsy whispered.

Brainy knew this game of charades wasn't going to get them anywhere. He whispered, "No one ever understands your hand signals, Hefty!"

⋆ The Lost Village ⋆

Frustrated, Hefty said, "Aggghhh! Never mind. Just follow me. And stay close."

The boys snuck across the floor and climbed up toward Smurfette.

Gargamel didn't notice them. He was obsessed with the hat. He pulled on a thread, which made the entire thing unravel. Which was what he wanted to do. Waving his hand over the threads, Gargamel began to chant.

"Wort of worm, and hair of cat," he intoned, sprinkling ingredients into a cauldron.

Azrael did a double take when he saw the hair. When had Gargamel taken a patch of fur off him?

"Show me the home of this Smurf hat!"

After all the ingredients were combined, there was a major magical reaction.

A disembodied voice boomed from the cauldron. "Long you have searched for these creatures of blue, but this hat comes from somewhere new."

Rubbing his hands together happily, Gargamel shouted, "Yes! Where?! Where does it come from?!"

The cauldron went on. "A village of Smurfs, where enchantment grows ..."

This was better than Gargamel ever dreamed. "An entire village? Go

Chapter 4 Gargamel's Evil Plan

on!"

"PLEASE STOP INTERRUPTING," the cauldron scolded.

"Okay, sorry ... Please continue."

"The location of which ... "

The wizard bent in to make sure he heard the directions clearly. "Yes?"

"Nobody knows." That was the cauldron's final answer.

"NOOOOO!!! Just start with that! Start with 'I don't know'! Lousy, cheapo cauldron!" Gargamel kicked the big black pot, hurting himself in the process. "Ow-hoo-hoo-hoo!"

The kick made the cauldron speak again.

"But here is a clue ... "

The Smurf hat thread floated to the surface of the potion and began to form a shape.

"Fascinating. What is it? I've got it. Three finger puppets with really big, puffy hair!" Gargamel nodded as he considered the image.

"Meow, meow," Azrael said. They were obviously trees.

"Trees? Must be a symbol for something, or a code," he muttered to himself, trying to decipher the code.

Azrael was already moving toward the map that was hanging on the wall. "Meow, meow, meow!" Azrael pointed, waving a paw frantically to a spot on the map.

⋆ The Lost Village ⋆

Gargamel was annoyed. "Azrael, it's not your map. If you want your own map, we'll get you your own map! But this is my map ... " Just to get the cat to stop, he gave in and went to look. "Wait a minute. Look what I found." He pointed with his wand. "Three Tall Trees! In the Forbidden Forest."

Azrael rolled his eyes. He did all the work and never got any credit!

"We've never searched there before. I'm a genius! Azrael, it's time to take a road trip!"

Frustrated and annoyed, Azrael refused to help as the wizard began to pack a bag.

While Gargamel was distracted, the Smurfs worked quickly to pick the lock on Smurfette's cage. They didn't have much time. The wizard was dashing back and forth across the lab, preparing for his "trip."

When Gargamel stopped at the cage, they had to rush to hide.

"Oh, Smurfette, congratulations! You've just led me to an undiscovered population of Smurfs!"

This was terrible! Smurfette shook her head.

"They have no idea we even exist!" Gargamel was so pleased. "I'll be like ... " He pretended he was sneaking up and attacking.

"And they'll be all ... " He made a surprised face.

"And I'll go ... " He moved his hands, as if there was a mighty explosion.

"And then they'll be like ... " He made a terrified expression. Then, with an echoing laugh, Gargamel leaned down, looking directly at Smurfette.

"At last, I'll have all the Smurfs I need to harness their magic and become infinitely more powerful! You little evil genius. The rotten apple doesn't fall too far from the tree after all." He smiled to himself and then went back to the map. "Get your fur and feathers in gear, boys!" Gargamel told Azrael and Monty. "We'll leave at first light, right after breakfast, say eight or eight thirty ... Nine at the latest!"

Gargamel then turned back to continue formulating his plot. That was Team Smurf's cue; they finally managed to bust the lock and set Smurfette free.

"Wait, Brainy—the map!" Smurfette whispered, and pointed.

"I'm on it," Brainy said with a wink. Using Snappy Bug, he took a bunch of photographs of the map on Gargamel's wall. They were going to need them.

Gargamel kept revising his schedule. "Barring any light packing and last-minute potty breaks ... "

He reevaluated the departure. "Fine, maybe nine thirty. Absolutely no later than ten, though!" Feeling satisfied, he rotated on his heel to see how his prisoner was doing, but the cage was empty!

"WHAT THE—" Gargamel's voice boomed.

There! Gargamel spotted Smurfette and the boys running for the

⋆ The Lost Village ⋆

window.

"It's a jailbreak!" he exclaimed. "No—they know my plans! They'll ruin everything!"

The Smurfs had to act fast. Hefty instructed the others to climb onto Gargamel's crossbow bolt.

"Is this safe?" Brainy asked.

"Well, it's a giant crossbow so I'm gonna go with NO!" Hefty took a seat.

"Don't let them escape!" Gargamel shouted.

Azrael dashed across the room, claws drawn, anxious to catch the Smurfs.

Gargamel came at them from the other direction.

The Smurfs were cornered, but just when it seemed like they would surely be caught, the mouse that'd been frozen before returned for its revenge. It pushed a Freeze Ball off the shelf, which hit Gargamel, freezing him in midair.

The wizard couldn't move. "Get them! Get those Smurfs!" He told his minions.

"Uhhhh, where are the seat belts?!" Smurfette turned, wide-eyed, to Hefty.

He told her to hang on and then announced, "Fire in the hole!" And with that, he kicked the crossbow trigger hard. Team Smurf went sailing through the air, down the hall, and out the cat door.

Monty chased them. He flew out of the front of the lair but didn't make it far before he smacked into a fence door.

"GET THOSE SMURFS!" Gargamel was still frozen.

Azrael zoomed past Monty. He turned back briefly to see Monty's head stuck.

"Meow," Azrael said, clearly meaning "You dumb bird."

The Smurfs quickly crossed the rickety old wooden bridge leading from the wizard's home.

Smurfette glanced over her shoulder. "Azrael's gaining on us!"

Monty had freed himself and was overhead as well. The bird took a nosedive at the bridge.

"Incoming bird!" Clumsy warned the others.

Monty crashed hard. He hit the bridge at such a high speed, it split the wooden planks in two. The Smurfs were holding on to one end. Azrael was hanging from the other.

"This might hurt!" Hefty warned as the bridge swung like a rope toward the rocky cliffs ahead.

"WWAAAAAAAHHHH!!!!!" Clumsy's scream went on and on.

The Smurfs slammed into the mountainside.

"OOF!" Clumsy lost his grip and fell. His scream continued. "AHHHHHHHHHHH!"

* The Lost Village *

Team Smurf all looked nervously down, only to discover they were only a few inches off the ground. Clumsy wasn't falling at all. He was lying flat on a rock below them—still screaming in panic.

Brainy, Smurfette, and Hefty hopped down and helped Clumsy up. Then they scampered away.

"Come on! Smurf this way!" Hefty took the lead.

At the top of the cliff, on the other side of the ravine, Azrael climbed to the edge of the cliffside, where he watched them get away.

Azrael called to Monty and pointed in the Smurfs' direction. "MEOW!! MEOW!"

Monty took off and soared over the Smurfs, but they ducked into an opening in the rocks to hide.

"Dohhohohohohoho!" Monty shrieked.

"RUN FASTER!! RUN FASTER!" Smurfette yelled.

"WHY ARE OUR LEGS SO SHORT?!" Brainy complained.

"WHY ARE OUR FEET SO BIG?!" Clumsy said as he tripped for the millionth time.

"WHY ARE MY MUSCLES SO BIG?" shouted Hefty.

"REALLY, MAN?" Brainy yelled.

"Dohhohohohohoho!" Monty hooted as he dove at them again.

At last, they reached the old hollowed-out log entrance to Smurf Village. Hefty, Brainy, and Smurfette dashed inside, but Clumsy tripped and was left outside the hidden entry, hanging from the edge of the log. Monty was headed straight for him.

"Um, guys! A little help here?" Clumsy's voice was tight with fear.

Monty was getting closer and closer!

He called louder, "He's coming! He's coming!"

Hefty dashed back and grabbed Clumsy, hoisting him over his shoulder and then running to safety. The log teeter-tottered over just as Monty overshot the distance and toppled right into a rock.

"Dohhohohohohoho." Monty shook off the fall and scanned the whole area. He was confused— Where'd they go?

The Smurfs were so happy to be home. They cheered and high-fived and hugged one another saying, "Woo-hoo!" and "Yeah!" and "All right!"

They'd have gone on celebrating all day, but then they noticed Papa Smurf was standing there, glaring at them, arms crossed over his chest. "Well, I know four Smurfs who have some explaining to do," he said.

Their cheers turned into worries. "Oh boy," Hefty muttered.

"That's not good," added Brainy.

Clumsy smiled meekly. "Hi."

Chapter 5 Secret Action of Team Smurf

The members of Team Smurf were speaking all at once, trying to explain to Papa what had happened.

It sounded like a jumble of words, and it was impossible to tell who was saying what:

"Oh my gosh, Papa, you won't believe it!"

"Smurfboarding!"

"Out of nowhere—mystery Smurf!"

"He lost his hat!"

"Ran into the Forbidden Forest!"

"Could be another village!"

"A giant vulture swooped down!"

"Locked in a cage!"

"Gargamel had Freeze Balls!"

"He had a map!"

"Gargamel is going to get them!"

"We have to go to the Forbidden Forest!"

"Three Tall Trees!"

"We got there just in time!"

Chapter 5 Secret Action of Team Smurf

"Hefty saved us all!"

"Hefty shot us out on a crossbow!"

The way they were telling it, Papa Smurf couldn't understand the whole story. "One at a time—one at a time! Please! Please!" Finally, he whistled loudly to get them to stop. It worked.

From the bits he gathered, he said, "I've told you time and again, the Forbidden Forest is forbidden!" He shook his head. "And now you're talking about maps and mystery Smurfs and Gargamel's lair!"

Hefty looked like he had something to say, but Papa wasn't about to let them start explaining again. He went on. "None of what you're saying makes any sense! And I really don't understand why you can't follow simple rules. You snuck out, and it put you all in danger! Seems to me the only way I can keep you safe is if you're grounded!"

Hefty, Clumsy, and Brainy immediately started complaining:

"Grounded?!"

"WHAT?!"

"That's not fair!"

"But, Papa!"

"Come on!"

Papa Smurf wouldn't listen to their excuses. This was serious. "No buts! None of you are to take one step out of your mushrooms without telling me where you're going. Do you understand that?"

⋆ The Lost Village ⋆

Smurfette knew Papa was serious. There was no way they'd convince him to let them go after Gargamel. Better to take the punishment and then find a way out of it.

"You're right, Papa," Smurfette said.

Papa didn't believe his blue ears! "Huh? What?"

"HUH? What?" Brainy and the others echoed.

Smurfette glared at the boys. "You're right. I don't know what we were thinking."

Papa gave her a long look, then said, "Uh ... good. Because as I was saying ... you all behaved completely irresponsibly!"

"Yes! Right! Exactly! Couldn't agree more. Right, guys?!" Smurfette was taking charge. There was no time to waste.

The boys were baffled. They started talking at the same time again:

"Right?"

"Excuse me?"

"Uh, What are you talking about, Smurfette?"

Papa regained his composure. "Yes, so, and furthermore—"

Papa was preparing to continue his lecture about their irresponsible behavior, but Smurfette cut in. "In fact, I think we should all go to our rooms right now and think about what we've done."

"Well, I think that's—"

"Tough but fair," Smurfette finished. She started to usher her friends

138

Chapter 5 Secret Action of Team Smurf

out the door, pushing and pulling to prod them along. "C'mon, guys."

"What's your endgame here, Smurfette?" Brainy asked.

"Okay, okay, I'm moving." Clumsy stumbled forward.

"Did you get pecked on the noggin?" Hefty wanted to know.

"Actually, Smurfette—" Papa had more to say.

Smurfette opened the door and gave the boys a shove outside. Looking back over her shoulder, she said, "Don't worry, Papa. We are certainly going to do some thinking about what we did. And so forth. And we will definitely not be leaving our rooms until we have thought this whole thing out. And then, for good measure, we'll think about it some more."

"Yes, but ... " Papa Smurf rubbed his beard.

"Great talk, Papa." She was the last to leave, and closed the door behind her.

Papa stood there for a beat, totally confused by what just happened, and then went back to his chair, saying, "I have no idea what I'm doing."

Smurfette felt bad about lying to Papa, but she knew in her heart that the other Smurf Village needed her help. When she got back to her mushroom, she filled her backpack with the essentials: water canteen, blanket, a flashlight, some snacks, and her hairbrush.

On the way out, she peeked in the mirror. That mirror reflected another mirror, which reflected itself, creating the image of infinite

* The Lost Village *

Smurfettes. With a confident nod, Smurfette snuck out.

Smurfette hurried to put distance between herself and Smurf Village. High above the hidden valley, she turned to look back one last time. There was no going home until she found the other village and warned its inhabitants about Gargamel.

Feeling a bit nervous about her mission, she walked on until she reached a large stone wall, near where she'd discovered the strange Smurf hat. She quickly found the tiny opening that she'd seen the other Smurf go through. With a deep breath, she began to enter when suddenly, Smurfette heard something rustling in the bushes. She stopped in her tracks, filled with fear, but then she realized what—or who—had made the noise.

"Hefty," Smurfette said. "I know that's you."

He stepped out.

"'Sup, Smurfette," he said, just as more rustling came from the bushes behind him.

"Brainy?" Smurfette said before she saw him.

"How'd you do that?" he asked.

She smiled. "And I assume Clumsy ..."

With a whoosh and a thud, Clumsy fell from a high tree, landing near Hefty.

"What are you guys doing out here?" Smurfette asked as Clumsy

Chapter 5 Secret Action of Team Smurf

dusted himself off.

"We knew you were up to something," Hefty told her.

"This is all my fault, Hefty," she explained.

"But, Smurfette, the Forbidden Forest?" Hefty moved into her path, blocking the way. "It's too dangerous."

She knew he was right. "I have to at least warn that lost village."

"Well, we're Team Smurf, and we stick together so ... " Hefty moved aside and stood next to her. "We're going with you."

"I can't ask you to do that," she protested.

"You didn't ask. We volunteered," Hefty replied.

"We volunteered," Clumsy agreed.

Smurfette quickly understood this was one fight she'd never win. Her friends would have her back no matter what. "Thanks, guys."

"First things first," Brainy said. He placed Snappy Bug down on a sheet of paper, and all the Smurfs gathered 'round as she drew them a map. It was just like the map they'd seen in Gargamel's lair, featuring three tall trees!

Clumsy was impressed. "Wow. Bug technology. Cool."

Brainy studied the drawing. "According to my map, we should be ... " He glanced around. "Standing right in front of this very large, tall stone wall."

They looked around and saw the stone wall looming over them.

⋆ The Lost Village ⋆

"Check!" Brainy said.

Hefty was going to take the lead, going first through the hole in the wall, but Smurfette stopped him. She took a deep breath and went in, her friends following close behind...

Chapter 6 Entered the Forbidden Forest

The Forbidden Forest was uncharted territory for the Smurfs in Smurf Village, so as Brainy saw it, they were conducting groundbreaking research! He didn't want to miss a thing, so he immediately began to record his thoughts with the help of Snappy Bug.

"One small step for four small Smurfs," he said proudly ... before stepping right into a spiderweb. "Ahhhh! Yuck!"

Smurfette couldn't believe her eyes. Everything was bright and colorful and smurftastic! "Wow, wow, wow, wow, wow ... WOW!" she gasped. She ran from rock to bush to plant, checking it all out. "AHHHH!"

Smurfette was gobbled up by a large flower.

Hefty rushed over, shouting, "Smurfette! You okay, Smurfette?"

Both Hefty and Brainy got close enough to also be gobbled up.

Clumsy was alone. Very slowly, he approached the flower. "Nice flowers ... Nice flowers ... "

All the flowers nearby started bending toward him, surrounding him. "NOT NICE FLOWERS!!!" he shrieked. Quickly turning, Clumsy tried to bolt away, but he ran right into the open mouth of a flower he hadn't noticed.

* The Lost Village *

Team Smurf was chewed up, spit out, and then gobbled up again, as the flowers each checked them out by tasting them.

"Ahhhhh! Ahhhhhhh! Ahhhhhh!" Brainy screamed every time his flower opened its mouth.

Then all at once, the flowers decided they didn't like the flavor of Smurf and spit them out one by one, hurling them deep into the Forbidden Forest.

Smurfette, Hefty, and Brainy each landed with a thud, covered in gooey, slimy plant saliva, but still in one piece.

Smurfette looked around. "Where's Clumsy?"

A second later, Clumsy shot out of the carnivorous flower. He plucked a leaf from a nearby plant to finish cleaning his face. Of course, this was a Boxing Plant, which started throwing punches like nobody's business. Clumsy took a direct hit to the nose and fell backward, rolling down a hill.

"Watch out for the steep embankment!" Brainy said, a second too late.

When the rest of Team Smurf found Clumsy, he was lying in the soft grass, eyes closed.

"Clumsy? You okay?" Smurfette asked.

He opened his eyes stared past her at some tiny glowing lights far above. "I'm seeing stars," he said.

Chapter 6 Entered the Forbidden Forest

Floating all around them were giant, iridescent winged insects.

"Wowwww!" the Smurfs all exclaimed together. The bugs filled the sky.

One of them swooped down.

"It looks friendly." Clumsy reached out toward the biggest one. In baby talk he asked, "What's your name?"

The big bug sniffed Clumsy's hat, then let out a "sneeze", followed by a burst of fire from its mouth. The tip of Clumsy's hat turned black from smoldering flames.

The other Smurfs moved in for a closer look.

Brainy was thrilled. He flipped through a book. "Amazing—a winged, fire-breathing Anisoptera. Let's see ... how should we classify this?"

Snappy Bug helped, making suggestions in cute, little squeaking noises.

"Hmmm, maybe. It seems like an easy choice," he replied. "But I'm just not sure."

"How about dragon ... fly?" Smurfette suggested, because of the way it breathed fire.

"Yeah. Okay. Let's go with dragonfly," Brainy concluded.

Clumsy stepped carefully away from the big bug. "Hopefully, it's more fly than dragon."

⋆ The Lost Village ⋆

Suddenly, the dragonfly grabbed Clumsy by the head and carried him off!

"Nope! Less fly! LESS FLYYYYYYYY!" he screamed when he saw that he was being taken to the dragonfly's nest.

His friends laughed, but Clumsy didn't find it funny at all.

"Uhhh, guys!" The dragonfly dropped Clumsy into the nest with her other eggs and then sat down on him to keep him warm. He tried to reason with the dragonfly. "I'm okay! A little help here?"

Down below, Gargamel, Azrael, and Monty made their way through the opening into the Forbidden Forest. They were also swept up into the flowers' mouths and spit out the same way.

"AHHHHH!! OOF! Ohhh." Gargamel swatted at his bird, who landed on top of him.

"Dohhohohohohoho," Monty replied.

"Monty, get off of me!" the wizard shouted. They were all covered in goopy flower nectar. "Argh! I hate nature! Oh gawdy!"

One of the Smurf-tasting plants hissed and snapped Gargamel's nose.

"AHHHH!!!! Azrael, do something! Stop laughing! This is not funny!"

Another plant grabbed the wizard's ankles.

Gargamel was furious. "Grrrr, wretched Forbidden Forest ... " This

Chapter 6 Entered the Forbidden Forest

was not going well.

Azrael sat safely to the side, purring and laughing.

Monty couldn't help because he was having his own issues with some sort of odd eyeball plants.

"Let—me—go!" Gargamel told the flowers. They did, spitting him out with a heavy thunk onto the forest floor.

Team Smurf looked up to the sky, where high above them, a moving canopy of hundreds of Dragonflies flew through the air. The sun reflected through their iridescent wings. In the trees hung hundreds of nests.

"These nests are made of some material I've never seen before," Brainy said, looking around.

"WHOA! OOF!" Clumsy managed to escape the dragonfly nest to join the group. "You know, I think I've had enough of these dragonfly for one day."

Suddenly, a shadow passed above, one that clearly wasn't a dragonfly.

It was Monty, and he was blocking their path!

The Smurfs turned to run, but Azrael was in the way, licking his lips with a fearsome "Meow!"

And finally, from behind a boulder stepped a sinister, smiling Gargamel.

⋆ The Lost Village ⋆

"Hey! What are you doing here?" Clumsy asked, a little baffled by the wizard's presence.

"I was thinking of getting a place out here, just a quiet place in the forest. It's a little breezy on the hill ... What do you think I'm doing out here, idiot?" Gargamel growled sarcastically.

"You are never going to find that village, Gargamel!" Smurfette said.

Gargamel laughed at her. "Oh, Smurfette! If it weren't for you, I wouldn't even have known about those other Smurfs. Get 'em, boys!"

At that, Monty and Azrael charged toward the Smurfs.

"Smurfentine formation, go!" Hefty shouted, and the Smurfs scattered.

Azrael and Monty smashed into each other.

Clumsy ran around Gargamel's feet screaming "Smurfentine", which confused the wizard long enough for Hefty to smack Gargamel in the shins with a branch.

"AHHHH!" the wizard shrieked.

Brainy dodged Azrael. "Smurfentine!"

"Smurfentine!" Smurfette shouted as she ran in the other direction.

Gargamel was spinning. Smurfs were attacking him from all angles. He tipped his head back and accidentally knocked an egg out of one of the dragonfly nests. Before it could fall too far, he caught it. The

Chapter 6 Entered the Forbidden Forest

dragonflies above were angry and agitated, giving Gargamel an evil idea.

He looked at Clumsy. "Hey, you! You're the clumsy one, right?"

Clumsy stopped running. "Huh?"

"Think fast!" Gargamel tossed the egg into Clumsy's arms.

"I caught it!" Clumsy looked at the egg and then at the angry Dragonflies. "This isn't good... "

The Dragonflies were now all focused on Clumsy! They swarmed around him and the other Smurfs.

"Clumsy! Give 'em back their egg!" Hefty ordered.

"Okay," Clumsy replied. He wanted to get rid of the egg, but no matter what he did, it ended up back in his hands. "Oh, come on," he muttered as the situation got more and more desperate.

"Clumsy!" Hefty shouted.

"I'm trying," Clumsy said as a dragonfly flame nipped at his butt. "YEOOOWWW!"

"Over there!" Smurfette shouted, seeing some rabbit holes up ahead that they could hide in. They all made a mad dash for safety.

Smurfette jumped into one of the holes in the ground. The rest of Team Smurf was right behind her.

"I'm sorry I poached your egg!" Clumsy set the egg on the ground as he leaped into the nearest hole. A dragonfly swooped in and grabbed the egg, and then, working together, other dragonflies blew fire into the

★ The Lost Village ★

rabbit holes.

Gargamel, Azrael, and Monty laughed with joy.

"Ha-ha! Well, they're dead." Gargamel rubbed his hands together gleefully.

"Meow, meow." Azrael wasn't so sure. "Meow!"

Gargamel argued, saying, "Ahh, it doesn't matter. What are a few worthless pennies when there's a pot of gold at the end of my rainbow?"

"Meow," Azrael countered, making his point.

"Oh, Azrael, I haven't had this much fun since we renovated the hovel."

"Meow."

"Can it, fuzzball! They're dead!" the wizard replied firmly.

"Meow, meow, meow," Azrael continued arguing as they began heading back toward the path.

"DEAD, I say!" Gargamel insisted.

"Meow, meow, meow." Azrael tried to get the last word, but the wizard ignored him.

Chapter 7 Inside the Rabbit Warren

Inside the rabbit warren, Team Smurf was still in one piece— Well, each Smurf was in one piece, anyway. The gang had been split up, with each Smurf pushed into a different, cavernous tubelike passageway. They were all alone, desperately searching for the others.

Brainy felt around in the dark for an exit.

"Hello?" Smurfette called.

"Smurfette?!" Hefty answered her.

"Echo! Echo! Echo!" Clumsy called out into the darkness. "I, uh— don't do well in the darkness," Clumsy said, his voice trembling. "I have enough trouble in the daylight!"

Brainy took charge, shouting through the tunnels. "Hold on, everyone. We need to find a way out of here."

"Wow! That is good thinking, Brainy." Hefty snorted. Obviously they needed to find a way out, but first they needed to find one another.

"Guys ... ?" Smurfette called to the others.

"Darkness!" Clumsy said, a bit more panicked this time. Where was everyone?!

Hefty tried to calm him down. "Don't be scared; just think happy

* The Lost Village *

thoughts."

"It's not really happy times right now," Clumsy countered.

"Just stay in the light, Clumsy," Smurfette suggested.

There were some small rays of light coming from breaks in the ground. He could see them up ahead.

"Too late." Clumsy was too scared to calm down. "I'm walking into the darkness."

"What? Why are you—Why?" Hefty just wanted them all to stay still.

"I'm really freaking out, you guys!" Clumsy snapped back.

"Stop!" Brainy called out before Clumsy could go too far. Brainy had prepared for this. "Everyone go into your backpacks, get out your Emergency Tunnel Survival Kit. Find the small glass vial marked 'light' and shake it."

Clumsy found a jar in his pack. He shook the jar gently, and a firefly inside lit up. Now he could see the path through the lonely tunnel.

Brainy checked in on his nervous friend, shouting, "Clumsy? How you doin'?"

"Uhhh. Okay, I guess," Clumsy said, staring at the firefly light as he searched through the pack to see what else Brainy had packed.

"Just hang tight, Clumsy. I'm not sure how long this'll take or how long we'll be down here. So, everybody, whatever you do, don't eat all

Chapter 7 Inside the Rabbit Warren

your rations!" Brainy really had thought of everything.

"I just ate all my rations!" Clumsy cried, dropping the wrappers to the ground.

"Clumsy!" Hefty said, rolling his eyes.

"I'm stress eating!" Clumsy was out of control.

Smurfette shouted, "I'm coming, Clumsy! Follow the sound of my voice—"

"Wait!" Brainy cut in, trying to stop her. "These tunnels are like a maze; we'll just get more lost."

"We gotta do something!" Smurfette said back.

"I'm with her—time for some action!" Hefty was ready to head out on his own.

"We're doing this all wrong," Brainy said. But he didn't have a better idea—yet.

"Smurfette?!?" Clumsy called her name into the dark.

"I'm close Clumsy, almost there!" Smurfette told him.

"That's just the echo playing tricks on us," Brainy warned.

Clumsy continued to panic. "Anybody?!"

"I'm here, I'm here, right around this corner." Smurfette turned down another tunnel.

"Hey, everybody! My light is going out." Clumsy's voice was shaking.

⋆ The Lost Village ⋆

Smurfette continued down the way she thought she heard him. "Clumsy?!" Her voice echoed.

Hefty heard the distress in Smurfette's voice. "That's it, I'm punching us outta here!" He began violently pummeling the wall with his fists. "Hwah! HWAH! HWAH-HWAH-HWAH!"

The ceiling above Smurfette began to crumble. "It's collapsing!"

"Hefty! Put those fists away before you get us killed!" Brainy shrieked.

"At least I'm trying something!" Hefty took another hit at the wall.

"I'm gonna blow us outta here," Clumsy said. He'd found an exploding energy drink in his pack.

Brainy shouted, "No!"

"Yeah!" Hefty loved the idea.

"Don't!" Smurfette said.

"Too late!" Clumsy tossed the energy drink into the tunnel wall and KABOOM!

"Clum ... sy?" Smurfette found him. Finally, they were together.

But the celebration was short-lived. Beady eyes filled the dark tunnel, every one of them fixed on the four Smurfs. Suddenly, the ground began to rumble, and out of the darkness, a stampede of green bunnies flooded the caves.

Smurfette began to run, then jumped up onto a bunny, as if it was an

Chapter 7 Inside the Rabbit Warren

oversize horse. "Wahhhhhahahahahahahhaaaaa!"

"Hey, Smurfette!" She looked over to see Clumsy riding a bunny too.

Smurfette followed him through the warren.

Brainy and Hefty each captured their own rabbits. When Hefty passed Clumsy, he grabbed him so they rode together on his rabbit. "Whoa! Ha-ha! Hang on, Clumsy bro! I got you, little buddy."

Riding "bunnyback", the Smurfs burst out of the underground labyrinth.

The frenzied herd of bunnies charged out after them, swarming from the tunnels and into the forest.

"STAMPEEEEEDE!" Brainy shrieked.

Clumsy, still riding with Hefty, was feeling a little ill. "I think my rations are coming up!"

Next to them, Smurfette was looking like a pro. Her bunny reared up on its hind legs and released a sort of rabbit-horse sound. Then it sped up, lunging forward and skillfully banking off trees along the way and sailing farther ahead.

Hefty and Clumsy weren't having such an easy time— They quickly got bucked off their bunny and landed on the back of Smurfette's. Brainy landed on hers too, but he was facedown, backside up. His glasses came to rest on his tail, making his butt look like a face.

* The Lost Village *

"What?!" Brainy asked, not understanding why everyone was laughing. "What's so funny?!"

"Now that's what I call 'talking out of your butt.'" Hefty laughed so hard he was tearing up.

As Brainy tried to regain his dignity, Smurfette noticed something in the distance. "Oh, boooyyyyyyys!" She pointed with joy. "Would anyone be interested in knowing that we are in sight of the Three Tall Trees?"

"Woo-hoo!" They cheered.

Smurfette patted her bunny on the back of his neck. "And Bucky is going to get us there extrafast!"

"Bucky?" Clumsy asked.

"Seems like a Bucky to me. Look at his teeth!" She gave him a little kick like he was a horse. "Hit it, Bucky!" She giggled as Bucky zoomed them closer to their goal.

Meanwhile, back in Smurf Village, Papa went to visit Smurfette at her mushroom. He knocked, but there was no answer from inside.

He spoke through the door. "Smurfette? Before you say anything, just listen. Now, I know yesterday I might've been a bit tough on you and the boys. And I know there are times I'm a little overprotective."

There was no response from inside, so he went on.

"Okay, a lot overprotective. But you have to understand—you

snuck out. You have to be more careful!" He was upset, but he stopped for a long moment to collect himself. "Smurfette, I know lately you may not realize it, and I may not say it enough, but you are— You shine. So, anyway, we're smurfy? I think you and your brothers have been grounded long enough." He expected her to come out, happy to hear that her punishment was over.

Instead, there was no reply.

"Smurfette?" Papa asked again. "Okay, I'm opening the door, and I'm walking in to talk more. You there? Smurfette?" He twisted the doorknob and slowly entered Smurfette's mushroom. It was immediately obvious she wasn't there. He was at first shocked, and then he became suspicious.

Papa went to Hefty's mushroom. "Hefty!" He rushed to Hefty's bed—it looked like Hefty was in it. But Papa pulled back the covers to find it was just a barbell.

"Brainy!" At Brainy's house, it looked like Brainy was standing at his blackboard, but actually, it was a dummy made up of objects from Brainy's lab.

Papa was getting very angry as he went to Clumsy's mushroom. "CLUMSY!" He pulled back Clumsy's bedcovers and found three apples there. "Oh, that's not even convincing!" Papa said. The apples didn't look like a Smurf at all.

⋆ The Lost Village ⋆

Papa Smurf marched out of the mushroom and then announced, "When I find those Smurfs, I will ground them for a month of blue moons!"

Just then, Nosey strolled by the window. "Hmm, what's going on in here?" Papa slammed the window shut. "Hmm, well, all right."

Chapter 8 Started Fire, Camped out, Built Raft

Team Smurf rode the giant bunny, Bucky, together through the dense woods and vast valleys, in the direction of the Three Tall Trees. Day faded to night, when the moonlight cascaded through the treetops. The darker it got, the more Bucky began to glow like a giant bunny flashlight.

"Wow!" Smurfette exclaimed, looking around from the bunny into the forest, which was illuminated as well. "Have you ever seen something so beautiful?"

Hefty turned to face Smurfette, full of sincerity. "Every day, Smurfette. Every. Day."

"Don't be weird," Brainy chided, rolling his eyes.

"You don't be weird," Hefty said crossly in return.

It was very late when Bucky started to slow down, clearly hungry and sniffing for food.

Clumsy was mumbling in his sleep as they rode. Brainy let out a yawn.

"We can camp here for the night," Brainy said, gesturing to a clearing. They all rolled off Bucky and started stretching. "I'll start us a

* The Lost Village *

fire. Fetch me some firewood, would ya, Hefty?"

"Um, a 'please' would be nice," Hefty grumbled.

"Yes, it would, but I haven't earned my manners badge so get me some firewood." Brainy pointed to a thick stand of trees.

Hefty muttered to himself as he collected sticks while Brainy referred to the campfire-building chapter of his book.

"Clumsy, you okay?" Smurfette asked, sitting down beside him.

"Yeah, sure ... " Clumsy said, reflecting on the day. "It's been fun. Well, not tons of fun, but it had its moments. Kind of. You know what I'm trying to say." He finally sighed and admitted, "It hasn't been that much fun."

Hefty dropped a load of wood in front of Brainy.

"Well done, Hefty, well done," Brainy said. Then referring to the instructions in the chapter, he said, "All right. Step one: The wood should be stacked in a tepee-like structure." He stacked it. "Step two: I tap this flint with a rock and ... " Brainy tried, but nothing happened. A few small sparks sputtered into smoke. He tried blowing on the wood to ignite a spark, but still nothing.

"You're not even blowing on it; you're spitting on it." Hefty said.

"Hmmm, that's odd. Perhaps the wood you collected was damp, Hefty. According to my manual, it should spark right up." Brainy read the page again.

Chapter 8 Started Fire, Camped out, Built Raft

"Hey, I've got an idea." Hefty grabbed the manual and threw it onto the pile of wood and WHOOOOSH! The sticks instantly erupted into a huge bonfire that lit the surrounding area.

"No, no, no, no, no, no!" Brainy quickly reached into the fire and pulled out his smoking book, flustered.

"You know, you're right, Brain Man ... Your little book does come in handy," Hefty said, smiling.

Brainy was furious. "Shame ... shame on you. We'd be lost without this book."

Hefty started talking in a hoity-toity voice, imitating Brainy. "My name is Brainy. I'm the supersmart Smurf."

Smurfette laughed at Brainy and Hefty as she brushed Bucky's fur. They were acting like brothers, fighting and arguing over the silliest things.

Brainy checked his manual. "Okay, the damage is minimal, and the binding is still intact." He took a whiff. "Smells good."

The Smurfs settled in around the campfire, gazing up at the night sky. Bucky was having a dinner of carrots and grass.

"Just think, guys," Smurfette said, tucking her hands behind her head. "After all this time, while we've been going about our smurfy business back home, there've been other Smurfs out there, just like us."

"Or they could be nothing like us," Brainy said.

⋆ The Lost Village ⋆

"He's right. We should be prepared for whatever we find," Hefty said. "Those other Smurfs might not even be blue."

"Maybe they'll be orange," Clumsy said. "I like orange."

"What if they all wear glasses?" Brainy dreamed.

"Or have big, bushy mustaches?"

"What if they have scaly skin and sharp teeth?" Brainy shuddered at the thought.

"And giant claws and little beady eyes," Hefty added, causing Brainy to shiver even more.

Smurfette didn't buy it; she was still convinced the new Smurfs would be as great as her own friends.

Clumsy tried to make a shadow puppet in the firelight. But of course, Clumsy was terrible at shadow puppets, so he just flashed both hands in shadow up on the trunk of a tree. "What if they have ... HANDS!"

Team Smurf roared with laughter this time.

"Listen, they could be very different from us, but I was different. Papa found the goodness inside me," Smurfette told the others. "These Smurfs deserve the same change I was given. I need to do this."

"And we're gonna help you. We're Team Smurf, and we're in this together." Hefty gave her an awkwardly long smile.

Brainy moved around the others, holding out his Snappy Bug on a selfie-stick made from a regular stick. "Okay, everyone: smurfy selfie

Chapter 8 Started Fire, Camped out, Built Raft

time!"

Snappy played a recording that said, "Say 'blue cheese!'"

"Blue cheese!" they said together.

The photo showed all of them happy and smiling, but Clumsy had his eyes closed.

Before sunrise, they started moving again. The four Smurfs rode on Bucky's back, more comfortably now that they'd had some rest. Bucky leaped over a hill and then skidded to screeching halt!

The Smurfs climbed down to see what had surprised Bucky. "According to this, we should be arriving at a river," Brainy announced, his face still buried in the map.

"Check," the other Smurfs said. It was a river, but not just any river. The flow surged and swelled, undulating in an almost-hypnotic state. The water was so clear they could see schools of glowing fish and bioluminescent sparkles. It was enchanting.

Hefty blinked hard. "It's like a workout for my eyeballs."

They climbed onto Bucky's back, and Smurfette said, "Okay, Bucky. Let's see how fast you can swim. Hiiya!"

The bunny refused to move.

"C'mon, boy. You can do it," Smurfette encouraged him.

Nope. Bucky backed away from the river, shaking his head in fear.

"What's a little water?" Hefty didn't understand the bunny's

* The Lost Village *

reaction.

"What's that, Bucky?" Clumsy acted as if he understood bunny-language. "The river is unsafe and full of dangerous surprises at every bend?" Clumsy was pretty sure that's what the bunny meant.

Brainy didn't think that was right. "No, I didn't get any of that. Perhaps Bucky just doesn't swim."

Hefty looked around, analyzing the situation. "That's too bad. We'd get there so much faster."

Brainy had a brilliant idea. "Aha! Fear not, my intrepid Team Smurf." He pointed at another badge on his backpack. "I didn't earn this raft building merit badge for nothing!"

Brainy consulted his manual.

Snappy Bug drew up the plans.

Brainy started building. He sawed wood and pounded nails until he fist-bumped himself and said, "Boom! Nailed it!" The raft was finished, and it looked amazing!

"Impressive, Brainy!" Smurfette exclaimed.

They all started to pile on when Hefty stopped Clumsy. "Here." He grabbed a doughnut-shaped flower blossom from a nearby plant and placed it over Clumsy's head like a life jacket.

"Oooh, stylish and practical," Clumsy said as he admired it.

Now they were ready.

Chapter 8 Started Fire, Camped out, Built Raft

They each said their good-byes to Bucky and prepared to push the raft into the water.

"Let's launch this bad boy!" Hefty exclaimed, ready to get moving.

"Wait! Remember, this strange river may hold untold surprises," Brainy warned. "We must be cautious!"

"Cautious. Good point. And heave ... " Hefty started again.

But Brainy was still wary. "Wait! Currents can be unpredictable. We must be alert and vigilant."

"Vigilance. Good call. On three, two—"

"Wait!" Brainy cut in again. "We must make sure we always—"

"Beep, blop, blorp." Hefty talked over him in annoying sounds.

"Pay attention to the—"

"Bong, bong, bing, bang!" Hefty went on.

"Rate of speed of the—"

"Beep, bop, bingo, bango, bing, bing, bang, bop."

Brainy gave up.

"Okay." Hefty smiled, knowing he'd won. "And we're off! HEEEEAAVE-HO!"

They pushed the raft off the bank and into the river and then settled down for the ride.

Smurfette waved at Bucky, who was watching them nervously from the shore. "Don't worry; we'll be fine!"

⋆ The Lost Village ⋆

The entire team waved and called out, "Bye, Bucky! Thank you! We'll see you on the way back!"

Bucky nodded and waved his paw.

As the raft gained speed, Clumsy noticed a lever that read "Emergency". "Hey. What's this thing?"

"I wouldn't touch that if I were you," Brainy told him.

Clumsy sat on his hands, complaining, "Oh, now all I want to do is touch it."

"At this pace, Gargamel doesn't stand a chance!" Smurfette said as they barreled down the river.

The early morning sunlight created a calming, beautiful atmosphere, and yet, it was also too quiet and a little eerie.

Smurfette pointed at the map and said, "Look! If we follow this river, we'll be right on course—"

"Right on course to the end of our rainbow," Gargamel finished Smurfette's sentence, then laughed.

Chapter 9 Gargamel's Scam

"Gargamel!" Smurfette exclaimed the instant she saw the evil wizard.

Gargamel and his crew made their own raft out of a floating log. Azrael was using Monty like an outboard motor, the bird's tail dipped in the water for propulsion.

"Smurfs!" Gargamel couldn't believe his eyes. "I thought I left you for dead!"

Clumsy pinched his lips together and stared at the emergency lever on the raft. This certainly seemed like an emergency to him ...

"Gun it!" Gargamel ordered Monty.

"Hang on, Smurf crew!" Hefty told the others. The raft began to move faster in the water. They pulled ahead of Gargamel's log.

"What the—NO!" The evil wizard grabbed a stick from the riverbank. He shouted at Team Smurf, "Stop ruining everything. I'm the one who ruins things!" Then he began to paddle his log toward the Smurfs, trying to knock them over into the swirling river.

Hefty slammed his fist into Gargamel's stick until the weapon was nothing more than a nub in the wizard's hand.

★ The Lost Village ★

"What? Azrael, get me a bigger stick." He tossed the tiny piece of wood aside, then looked up. His eyes went wide with fear!

Team Smurf also panicked when they noticed what was right in front of them all.

It was Enchanted Rapids! A crazy, treacherous, and magical roller coaster ride of swirling water with bumps and spins.

"Oh dear," Gargamel gasped. Azrael meowed nervously as they got closer and closer.

"Clumsy! Pull the lever!" Brainy shouted.

"Seriously?! But you said not to! Is this a trick?"

"PULL IT NOW!" Brainy and Smurfette ordered at the same time.

Clumsy tugged at the emergency lever. A sailing mast immediately popped up.

The rapids sent Gargamel and his log flying into the air and underwater.

"WHAAAAAAAAAAA!" Gargamel shrieked.

Harnessing the wind into the raft's sail, Hefty easily steered them a safe distance away. But when they hit another rapid, Clumsy was thrown overboard. "Whoa!" He landed on Gargamel's log, running in place to keep from falling over.

Gargamel kept churning through the swiftly moving water, cursing as his head popped up and down.

Azrael lunged for Clumsy, but was knocked back by a huge wave,

Chapter 9 Gargamel's Scam

just as Clumsy was thrown safely back onto the Smurfs' raft. Team Smurf was fully engulfed in the rapids at this point, but they were working together to navigate.

"Look out!" Brainy called as he noticed a huge boulder coming their way.

Team Smurf ducked in time, but Gargamel didn't. The wizard and his pets saw the rock just before it hit them. Their log overturned, throwing Gargamel and his crew into the rapids.

"Meow," Azrael muttered.

"I love you, too," Gargamel said to his cat, just before a wave hit and they were both sucked under.

"Yeah! We did it!" the Smurfs shouted.

"Sink or swim!"

"Gargamel's toast!"

"Take that!"

Then, from behind, they heard a cry for help. It was Gargamel, struggling to stay afloat.

Brainy ignored him, saying, "All right! We're still on course!" In the distance, they could see the Three Tall Trees.

"Double-time it, Hefty!" Smurfette was excited they were so close, but with one last look behind them, she saw Gargamel still battling the rapids.

⋆ The Lost Village ⋆

"Help! I'm sinking! Please! I'm afraid of turtles!" Gargamel thrashed his arms.

"Um, guys, what's he up to now?" Clumsy asked the others.

Brainy wanted to keep moving. "Forget that guy!"

Gargamel begged them. "HELP! My cat can't swim!"

Suddenly, everyone on the raft got very quiet. All the Smurfs were staring at Gargamel, deciding what to do. Hefty was the first to speak up. "We gotta help him."

"Are you crazy? Why?!" Brainy demanded.

"Because it's what I do," Hefty said simply.

"Listen to him!" Gargamel said between gulps of air.

"But he's our sworn enemy!" Brainy reminded Hefty.

"He's literally a villain!" Clumsy added.

"I can change!" The wizard was splashing in the river a little more frantically now.

"And I literally wear my heart on my sleeve, okay?" Hefty turned to show them his heart tattoo.

"That's your shoulder. Not a sleeve," Brainy pointed out, rolling his eyes.

"I like your tattoo!" Gargamel called back.

Hefty couldn't let the wizard drown. "We're doing this." He began to turn the raft.

Chapter 9 Gargamel's Scam

"Smurfette, talk some sense into him!" Brainy pleaded with her.

Hefty glanced at Smurfette, who was debating the problem. "Brainy, I hate Gargamel more than anyone, but we're Smurfs. We do the right thing."

"Thank goodness for it," Gargamel said.

"We have to save him," Smurfette told the others.

"I just want to go on record that I'm decisively against this," Brainy said.

"Whatever, we're doing it." Hefty moved the boat closer to the wizard.

"Sounds awesome." Gargamel was anxious to be rescued.

Smurfette grabbed the doughnut-shaped blossom life vest from Clumsy and handed it to Hefty. "Here, use this!"

Hefty steered the raft into position and threw the flower. "Grab on!"

"I don't know about this." Brainy was worried.

Gargamel pulled himself up. "You won't regret it. Thank you, thank you, such a kind Smurf."

"Are you okay?" Hefty asked.

"I'm okay. Wet, tired, kind of waterlogged. Thanks for asking, but I'm still evil so ... " With a swipe of his hand, he knocked the Smurfs into the water and claimed their raft for himself. "Enjoy drowning!" He laughed. "Hope you're better swimmers than you are judges of a wizard's character!"

Monty and Azrael made themselves comfortable on the raft.

The Smurfs were separated in the churning waters. They floated for a few moments in the wild rapids, and then ... they disappeared over the edge of a cliff and down a massive waterfall.

"AHHHHHHHHHHHHHH!"

Smurfette, Hefty, Brainy, and Clumsy all disappeared into the mist.

Chapter 10 Arrived in the Lost Village

Smurfette was washed ashore in a blue lagoon. She landed facedown in the sand. Scattered nearby on the shore were Hefty and Brainy.

Smurfette sputtered and coughed. "Brainy?! Hefty?! You okay?"

Brainy choked out, "Define 'okay'."

Smurfette looked around for Clumsy. "Where's Clumsy?" she asked the others.

Hefty got up, brushed off the sand, and started calling, "Clumsy? Clumsy! Clumsy?" Brainy helped with the search.

The three Smurfs walked up and down the beach, calling his name.

"Uhhh, a little help here," a small voice called out. "I'm okay ... I think."

They found Clumsy buried in the sand, being attacked by crabs, but something was still wrong. Brainy began searching the beach, muttering and flipping out. "My pack! My manual! No! No! No! No!" He dug through a mound of sand. Angry, he turned to face Hefty. "This is all your fault!"

"WHAT?!" Hefty asked, hands on hips, ready to fight.

"Brainy, cut it out!" Smurfette stood with Hefty.

★ The Lost Village ★

Brainy quickly turned on her. "Oh, I'm sorry. Correction: It's your fault too!"

"Leave her out of this!" Hefty was furious.

"Hefty! I don't need you to fight my fights for me!" Smurfette told him.

"Oh great, so now you're mad at me?" Hefty asked her.

Brainy pointed angrily at Smurfette. "You're the one that got us into this whole mess in the first place!"

"Hey! I was ready to do this on my own," Smurfette shot back, reminding him of how she'd planned to make this journey alone from the beginning.

"Oh, well, then so much for Team Smurf!" Hefty threw up his hands. The gang was breaking up.

"I WANT TO YELL ABOUT SOMETHING!" Clumsy shouted, just to be like the others.

"Stay out of this, Clumsy!" Brainy now turned on him too.

"YELLING!!" Clumsy yelled back.

Hefty couldn't take it any longer. "That's it, Brain Man! It's time for you earn your manners badge." He charged after Brainy.

"Stop it!" Smurfette tried to break them up, but Brainy lunged at Hefty.

The fight had just begun when suddenly, dozens of arrows rained

Chapter 10 Arrived in the Lost Village

down on them. SHWOOP! SHWOOP!

"Take cover!" Smurfette shouted.

Hefty pulled them all together as they were encircled by a giant caterpillar-like creature that appeared from the bush.

The caterpillar disassembled, coming apart piece by piece. Each part was a small masked creature.

Clumsy fainted, face-first, into the sand.

One of the creatures stepped forward, as though curious. The rest of the creatures prodded the Smurfs forward, forcing them to march. Hefty carried Clumsy in his arms as they left the beach with their captors who were leading them into the woods.

Team Smurf was terrified. Would they ever get home again?

Suddenly, the creatures stopped. They gathered around the Smurfs with whispers of confusion and excitement.

One creature came closer to them. It felt threatening.

Hefty stepped forward, blocking his friends, trying to keep them safe. Smurfette peeked over his shoulder.

"Who are you? Whaddya want?" Hefty demanded to know.

"Her," the creature said, pointing at Smurfette.

All the masked creatures suddenly rushed up and started grabbing at Smurfette, touching her hair and examining her dress.

"Smurfette!" Hefty tried to push them back, but there were too many of them.

"Hey!" Smurfette batted their hands away.

"Look at that hair," one said.

"And that dress," said another.

"Funny shoes," a third creature laughed.

"She smells good."

"She looks weird."

The creatures went on and on, checking Smurfette out.

Pushing through the crowd, one creature came forward, coming face-to-face with Smurfette. They studied each other for a beat.

The creature was so familiar ... Smurfette gasped, "It's you!"

The creature ripped off its mask.

It was a Smurf. A girl Smurf. Just like Smurfette!

"You're a girl!" Smurfette jumped for joy and then told her friends, "She's a girl!"

Another creature took off her mask. Then another and another.

"Oh!" Smurfette said as she began to understand that they were all girls. "Ohhhhhhhhhh ..."

"This is her," the first Smurf told the others. "This is the Smurf I was telling you about."

A chorus of whispers rose up from the crowd. "The one from the wall? She's real."

Chapter 10 Arrived in the Lost Village

The first Smurf reached forward to pinch Smurfette's skin, examining her closely. "I'm Smurflily."

"Hi. I'm Smurfette," Smurfette replied.

One of the creatures removed her mask and leaped forward, nearly knocking Smurfette over while trying to hug her. "Oh my jeez-to-petes," she apologized. "I'm Smurfblossom. Nice to meet you! We don't have a Smurfette. But we do have ... " She took a big breath in and pointed at the others. "Smurfpetal, Smurfclover, Smurfmeadow, Smurfdaisy, Smurfholly, Smurfhazel—"

"Heeeey." A group of girls took off their masks and waved.

"Oh, everyone can just introduce themselves later." Smurfblossom waved them away and then spun Smurfette around. "Look at you! You're so different. I mean, sorry, but it's true. Do you know how to start a fire with just a rope and a stick? I do! I can show you. Actually, Smurfstorm can show you; she's the best at that kind of thing. Right, Stormy?"

Smurfstorm was not as enthusiastic about Smurfette as the others. She took aim at the Smurfs with her bow and arrow.

Smurfblossom didn't let Smurfstorm ruin the mood. "That means yes! Have you ever seen a rainbow? What about a double rainbow? What about an upside-down rainbow? So is your favorite song 'Hey, Hey, Hey, Hey, Hey! Hey, Hey, Hey, Hey, Hey, Hey, Hey!'? Mine is. Your dress is sooooooo pretty!"

⋆ The Lost Village ⋆

Smurfette was overwhelmed.

Smurflily told her to calm down. "Smurfblossom, remember, work on that filter, okay?"

Smurfblossom was too wound up for slow breaths. She breathed as fast as she talked.

Smurfstorm was more cautious than her sisters. She leaned forward into Smurfette's face. "What's your deal, anyway?"

"Oh, uh, well ... " Suddenly, it all came rushing back to Smurfette—the reason for her mission! She had to warn them, to protect them! "We came to warn you about Gargamel!" Smurfette blurted.

"Garga-what?" the girls all asked at once.

"He's a dangerous wizard who wants to capture all Smurfs and use them for his evil magic! And he knows about the lost village."

The girls gave one another a look.

"Lost village?" Smurfstorm fumed. "You're the ones who are lost. Not us."

"We have to take you to Smurfwillow," Smurflily told Smurfette.

Another girl asked about Hefty, Clumsy, and Brainy, saying, "What should we do with these blue blobs?"

Smurflily checked them out, then said, "Oh, ummm ... bring them along!"

"Come on, Smurfette!" Smurfblossom was so excited about their

Chapter 10 Arrived in the Lost Village

new friend. "Wait'll you see Smurfy Grove. I'm gonna show you my room, you can tell me all about Gargamel, and then I can braid your hair. Do you want hear my favorite song again? Hey, hey, hey, hey, hey, hey ... "

A tough girl Smurf pushed the boys forward. "All right, move!"

Clumsy stumbled on the path. "Wow. Girl Smurfs be bossy."

The Smurfs were led to Smurfy Grove. Trumpets sounded as they approached the entrance. The doors opened, and the members of Team Smurf found themselves looking out over the center of Smurfy Grove, surrounded now by one hundred girl Smurfs who were whispering and chatting.

"Who's the girl and what are those other things?"

"Oh, gross!"

"I think they're kinda cute, in a gross way."

"What are those?"

"The strange ones aren't wearing any shirts."

"I can see their tails!"

"Is there something wrong with them?"

"Are they sick?"

"Are they food?"

Stormy raised her weapon toward the boys.

Smurfette stood up, high on a box, and explained, "No, no, no ...

⋆ The Lost Village ⋆

They're Smurfs. Just like us. Except, well, they're boy Smurfs."

"BOY" was a new word, and it quickly spread through the grove, whispered from girl to girl.

"Boy," Smurfblossom repeated it. "That's a funny word. Boy, boy, boy, boy, boy, boy." She lowered her voice like the boys'. "Look at me, I'm a boy Smurf. Ha-ha-ha!"

Hefty, Clumsy, and Brainy gave one another a look. They were a little worried about where this was headed.

"Boys?"

"Where do they come from?"

"Ew!"

"So gross!"

"Boys—ick."

"Funny looking."

"Not that smart."

"They smell like soil."

"Sweaty."

"Why are their voices so low?"

"Are those pants attached to shoes or shoes attached to pants?"

"Where's their hair?"

"Where's their shirts?"

"I like what I see!"

Chapter 10 Arrived in the Lost Village

"I want to not like them, but I'm somehow drawn to them."

So many voices at once! They were crowding around the boys. One of them poked at Hefty's heart tattoo.

"Brainy's log, day two: We've encountered a rare, new life-form. They are at times very intimidating, and they smell nice. More on that later."

"Hello, boy," one of the girls said, starting to reach for him, but Brainy pushed her back.

"Boundaries! Okay! Ahh! Hey! That's enough of that!"

"They're my friends." Smurfette introduced them. "That's Hefty, Brainy, and Clumsy."

Clumsy waved. "Hey there!"

"Hooptie, Berney, Klutzy. Got it." Smurfblossom really didn't have the names down at all. "We should do name tags!"

"Wait. Where are ... all your boys?" Smurfette looked around. She hadn't seen any boys in the entire grove. Not yet, anyway.

Giggles filled the air.

"You won't find any boys here." A voice echoed through the square.

Everyone looked up to find a masked creature, standing on a balcony high above them. When she removed her mask, she revealed a face that was older, wiser—much like Papa Smurf. She slowly moved down a winding staircase made of vines, like an old lady. But then suddenly she

* The Lost Village *

jumped off the side, grabbing on to a spinning flower-copter and landing confidently next to Smurflily.

"I am Smurfwillow, leader of the Smurfs."

Smurfette was in awe.

Smurfwillow nudged her. "This is called an introduction, so now you go."

"Uh ... I, uh ... " Smurfette began.

Smurfstorm stepped in between Smurfwillow and Team Smurf. "Don't get too close, Willow," Smurfstorm warned. "Something's not right here."

Smurfette jumped in, "I promise, we're only here to help. We came to warn you about the evil wizard Gargamel. He has a map, with a landmark leading him to three tall trees. Show them, Brainy."

"Snappy," Brainy called. Snappy Bug popped out from under Brainy's hat.

Out of caution, Smurfstorm drew her bow, and trained it on Snappy. "Don't try any funny stuff, bug."

Snappy took a deep breath, marched past Smurfstorm, and drew the three tall trees in the dirt.

"I hate to break it to you, but those aren't trees," Smurfwillow told them.

Smurfette and the boys walked with Smurfwillow, where the view in

Chapter 10 Arrived in the Lost Village

the distance was clear, and looked out to where Smurfwillow was facing. She was pointing to the lagoon where they'd come from, and above it ...

"Waterfalls? They're waterfalls!" Smurfette considered the wizard's misunderstanding. "That means Gargamel is going the wrong way!"

"And if he went there"—Smurfwillow gestured toward the Three Tall Trees—"then that means the Swamp of No Return!" Smurfwillow was satisfied they were all safe. "There's no way he could survive."

Chapter 11 Gargamel Ran Away from Swamp

In the Swamp of No Return, Gargamel was indeed in deep trouble.

"Help me! Help me! There's no way we can survive!" the wizard shouted into the wind.

With Azrael on his head, Gargamel held on to his bird for dear life as he was attacked by vicious, enchanted piranhas.

Back in Smurfy Grove, Smurfette told Smurfstorm, "With all due respect, you don't know Gargamel." She knew that Gargamel could weasel his way out of even the most dire situations and that it was wrong to underestimate him.

"Yeah? Well, with no due respect, you don't know us," Smurfstorm told her.

Smurfblossom agreed. "Trust us, he's a goner!"

Smurfwillow suggested, "Stormy, why don't you do a little recon, check things out."

"And leave you with these four? No way! Look at that one!" Smurfstorm cried, narrowing her eyes at Hefty. "He can't be normal."

"I think we'll be just fine here," Smurfwillow replied calmly.

Chapter 11 Gargamel Ran Away from Swamp

With sigh and a sharp whistle, Smurfstorm called "Spitfire!" A dragonfly zoomed down from the treetops and landed nearby.

Smurfstorm climbed onto Spitfire's back and asked, "Okay, what does this Gargamel look like?"

"Oh, you know," Clumsy replied. "He's your typical male wizard—long black robe, lives alone with his cat and his bird. It's sad, really."

Smurfstorm made a quick decision and nodded toward Clumsy. "You're coming with me. You can point him out."

"Hey! Whoa, whoa, whoa!" Hefty tried to intercede. "There's no way he's getting on—"

But Smurfstorm snatched Clumsy before there could be any further discussion.

"Ahhhhh!" Clumsy shrieked as they lifted off the ground. "I feel the need to remind you, my name is Clumsy." The Spitfire rose higher into the sky. "WHOOOOOAAAAAA!"

"Clumsy!" Hefty called out as they disappeared over the horizon.

"Don't worry, Clumsy is in good hands," Smurfwillow told him.

Smurfblossom smiled. "Oh, Stormy is the sweetest! ... In her own way."

Once they were gone, Smurfwillow turned to the girls. "All right, girls, in the meantime, our guests have had a long journey, so let's show them some hospitality, Smurfy Grove style!"

⋆ The Lost Village ⋆

The girl Smurfs cheered and ran off in every direction. They were going to have a party!

Hefty, Brainy, and Smurfette were the center of attention at the welcome celebration.

There was music. Confetti and flower petals floated in the air.

They were given gifts: necklaces, bracelets, beads, feathers, leaves, flower crowns, and ornate head dressings. Hefty was awkward and unsure of all the new things and attention, but Brainy was intrigued by all the customs and different objects in Smurfy Grove. Smurfette was trying her best to take everything in. She was loving every inch of the grove and every minute of her time there.

After the initial celebration was over, Hefty, Brainy, and Smurfette split up to tour the different areas of Smurfy Grove.

In one of the shops, Brainy was explaining a long math problem to the girls, but he couldn't figure out why they were all laughing. It wasn't until he turned around that he saw Hefty drawing a fart cloud on the blackboard behind him.

Later, the girls took Hefty and Brainy to the gym. Hefty was trying his best to impress the girls by lifting the heaviest weights. Suddenly, a fart noise rang out every time he lifted a weight, and the girls broke into laughter. Brainy and Snappy Bug were using a whoopee cushion to get revenge!

Chapter 11 Gargamel Ran Away from Swamp

Still sour about what happened at the gym, Hefty took a seat in a circle of Smurf girls who were working together to make camouflage leaf quilts. Hefty kept poking himself with the needle as he tried to help; he was irritated but determined to get it right. A few hours later, Hefty's fingers were covered in bandages, but he held up a quilt that was surprisingly detailed and well-done. He smiled ... until Brainy held up an even bigger quilt of his own.

While Hefty and Brainy were off trying new things, Smurfwillow took Smurfette to the archery range. Smurfette was surprised to find out she was quite good at using a bow and arrow! After archery, Smurfette and some of the other girls went flower jumping. It was a little scary at first, but once she got the hang of it, Smurfette was whirling down the biggest tree in delight. The rest of the day was a blur—Tai Chi, basketball, even Spitfire riding!

At the end of the day, Smurfwillow showed Smurfette a huge mural of the girl Smurfs. Smiling, Smurfette painted herself into the picture. Her heart was bursting with joy and happiness at the freedom she was experiencing.

Smurfette wasn't sure she'd ever want to leave.

In the depths of the Swamp of No Return, Gargamel was still struggling to get out of the swamp. He grabbed Monty by the tail,

⋆ The Lost Village ⋆

demanding, "Flap, Monty! Flap vigorously! Use your mighty condor wings to carry your master to safety!"

A piranha bit Gargamel on the butt.

"OUCH! Sweet mercy! They're bottom-feeders! Ouch! Ah! Ah!" Gargamel grabbed one of the piranhas and decided to teach it a lesson. "Devil fish!"

Azrael noticed there were Smurfs flying above them. "Meow!"

Gargamel slammed the piranha into the ground, then yelled to Azrael, "WHERE. IS. MY. LOST. SMURF. VILLAGE?!"

"Meow!" the cat answered.

Gargamel looked up. "What?" High above them, he saw Smurfstorm and Clumsy. "Smurfs! Why won't they just die?! Monty, retrieve them!" Gargamel commanded his bird.

Monty flapped away to chase down Smurfstorm and Clumsy.

From far below, Smurfstorm and Clumsy hadn't seen Monty yet. They were still searching for Gargamel. Suddenly, Spitfire made a jerky swoop, causing Clumsy to hold on tight.

Clumsy was busy still trying to explain to Smurfstorm about the wizard. "Oh, he exists all right. He and his stinky cat and his doo-doo bird. They've been terrorizing us the entire journey. But he didn't like us from the start.

"He could never find our village," Clumsy continued. "So then he

Chapter 11 Gargamel Ran Away from Swamp

made a plan to capture us all. That's when Gargamel created Smurfette. Anyways—"

Smurfstorm hadn't really been paying much attention to Clumsy's rambling, but that last tidbit of information made her pause. "Hold up! Smurfette was created by this Gargamel?"

"Oh, yeah. From a lump of clay. Really cool story, actually." Clumsy smiled.

"I knew I didn't trust her." Smurfstorm frowned.

"You'd like her if you get to know her. She's just like you but nice," Clumsy said, about to go on when Smurfstorm noticed Monty flying toward them.

"Hold on! We gotta bogey coming in."

That made no sense to Clumsy. Smurfstorm reached out and physically turned his head so he could see Monty, headed straight for them.

"That's no bogey! That's Gargamel's big dumb bird!" Clumsy said, panic rising inside him.

"Here, you fly." She pushed Spitfire reins toward Clumsy.

"Uhhh, that's not a great idea," Clumsy said. "Flying's not really my thing."

"Have you ever flown before?" Smurfstorm asked.

"Well, no ... " Clumsy admitted.

⋆ The Lost Village ⋆

"Then how do you know it's not your thing?" Before he could protest again, Smurfstorm shoved the reins into his hands while she fired off shots with her bow and arrow. Through sheer dumb luck, Monty was able to avoid the arrows.

"He's coming back!" Smurfstorm warned Clumsy.

She had a stash of ammo ready to fire: berries, sticks, and rocks. But she would run out if they didn't shake the bird soon. "Hurry!" she told Clumsy.

"Uhhh. What do I do?" He had no idea what she meant. Accidentally, he caused Spitfire to swerve, just in time to dodge Monty's attack.

"Good move! Now, do it again!" Smurfstorm cheered.

"Ooookaaayyy ... " Clumsy wasn't sure he could do it again, but he was willing to try. With a tug on the reins, he managed to get Spitfire to spiral expertly into the air. "Hee-haw!" he cheered.

But Monty was still hot on their tails.

Having freed himself from the swamp, Gargamel was now standing at the murky water's edge, staring up at Clumsy. "Yeeessss!" Then he realized something important. "Wait a minute! I don't recognize that other Smurf!" He gasped. "It's a girl! They found my lost Smurf village!"

Clumsy ducked and dove Spitfire away from Monty. He passed another arrow to Spitfire. "Hey! I've got an idea! Spitfire, spit fire!"

Spitfire lit up the end of the arrow with flames, and Clumsy handed

Chapter 11 Gargamel Ran Away from Swamp

it back to Smurfstorm.

"I like the way you think," she said. She took the shot and hit Monty's wing.

"Ouch, ouch, ouch, ouch," Monty squawked, then fell out of the sky, injured. Gargamel ran to catch him.

"Monty!! What have they done to you my glorious bird of prey?" Gargamel shook his fist up at Spitfire. "SMMMUUUURRRFFF SSSS!!!"

"I can't believe he escaped the swamp! We have to warn the others!" Smurfstorm set a course for home.

"You hear that, Spitfire? Back to Smurfy Grove," Clumsy said, anxious to get as far away from Gargamel as possible.

Unaware of the danger approaching the grove, Hefty and Brainy were relaxing in a Smurf-spa. Hefty was wearing an organic facial mask. A caterpillar began using its many legs to give him a back massage.

"So ... interesting day," Brainy said, looking over at his friend.

"Yeah," Hefty said happily.

"You actually did math?" Brainy said.

"Not just math ... basic math," Hefty bragged.

Above them, there was a rustling sound as Smurfette floated down to them on a daisy.

* The Lost Village *

"Hey, guys! Isn't this place awesome?!" She looked radiant and happy, decked out in traditional Smurfy Grove clothing.

She was hanging out with Smurfblossom and a few other girl Smurfs.

"Doesn't she look great? It's like she's one of us now!" Smurfblossom said with a huge smile. "She should stay with us forever!"

Smurfblossom's words hit Hefty like a punch in the gut. He didn't want Smurfette to stay with them! She belonged with her friends in Smurf Village!

"Uhhh, one, she always looks great," he said. Then adding, "Two, this is gettin' a little outta hand, don't you think?"

Smurfette giggled. "Sorry. I can't take you seriously with that mask on your face."

Hefty yanked off the beads and feathered hat he was wearing and wiped his face.

Brainy slowly began to clean himself up too.

Hefty stood. "Smurfette, we did what we came here to do. These Smurfs know about Gargamel, so come on, let's start thinking about heading home." Despite himself, a bit of panic snuck into Hefty's voice. It was time to leave before they lost Smurfette to Smurfy Grove forever.

"Home? But I ... " Smurfette looked around at the village and the girl Smurfs who surrounded her. It was so perfect.

Chapter 11 Gargamel Ran Away from Swamp

"He's right, Smurfette. We've been gone almost two whole days. Papa Smurf's going to be very upset with us," Brainy said, reminding her where they really belonged.

"It's time to go," Hefty added.

Smurfette was quiet for a long moment.

"Smurfette!" Hefty said to get her full attention.

Just then a whirring noise made them all look up.

"We are here!" Clumsy announced from high in the sky. His friends stared in amazement as Clumsy explained, "Turns out—I do do well with Spitfire."

Smurfstorm was all business as she slid confidently off Spitfire and marched right up to Smurfette, who was standing with Smurfwillow.

"They were right. This Gargamel character ... He's real, and he's headed this way," Smurfstorm told them all.

"Oh no! See, I told you—" Smurfette began, but she was cut off by Smurfstorm.

"Put a cork in it, Smurfette. The way I see it, you and your little boy friends led him straight to us. But of course, that was your plan all along, wasn't it?"

"Smurfstorm, easy—" Clumsy protested.

Smurfstorm turned to the crowd, as though she were a lawyer presenting her case. "Little Miss Yellow Hair here isn't a real Smurf. She

★ The Lost Village ★

was created by Gargamel. The Clumsy blob told me so himself."

Smurfwillow put up a hand. "Smurfette, is this true?"

"I— It's not like that." Smurfette wanted to defend herself.

"She was made to help him find Smurfs!" Smurfstorm's eyes were filled with anger.

"Smurfette came here to help you. We all did," Hefty put in.

"It's okay, Hefty. This is all my fault." Smurfette looked around sadly. She'd been so happy here, and now things were turning ugly.

Just then, the village alarm sounded. The ear-piercing wail screeched through the town.

"Girls! Protection mode!" Smurfwillow commanded. The girl Smurfs disappeared into their homes and returned a moment later with weapons.

They stood, tense and ready, as a rustling sound came from the nearby bushes.

"Hold!" Smurfwillow told them, commanding her troops. "Hold!"

Suddenly, a blaze of red, blue, and green light burst through the leaves!

"NOW!" Smurfwillow leaped forward and attacked the intruder, pinning him to a tree.

Chapter 12 Gargamel Attacked the Smurfy Grove

Smurfwillow had captured Papa Smurf. He'd come into the village riding on Bucky.

Papa managed to break free and face his attacker. She was wielding a staff. But Papa had mean fighting skills. They were evenly matched. The battle between them went on and on until Smurfwillow stepped into a pool of light, allowing Papa to see that she was a Smurf!

For a second, he was so surprised that he was thrown off guard. That gave Smurfwillow time to take the lead and defeat him.

"Surrender, wizard!" she demanded.

"Wiz—What? Who are—?" Papa had no idea who he was facing or what she meant.

Girl Smurfs began to slowly emerge from behind trees and rocks. Papa was stunned.

The girls checked him out.

"Oh, he's so old," one said.

"Look at his face." Another leaned in close.

"Is he wearing a disguise?" A girl reached out toward Papa's beard.

★ The Lost Village ★

"He doesn't seem so tough," Smurfstorm said with a hearty laugh.

"Yeah, Gargamel! That's what you get when you attack Smurfy Grove!" Smurfblossom shouted, doing a happy victory dance.

"Gargamel? What are you—?" Papa didn't understand.

Smurfette worked her way through the crowd. "Wait! This is a mistake!"

"Smurfette?!" He was already confused. Now it was worse. What was she doing here?

"That's Papa!" Smurfette told the group.

"Papa? There's another funny word," Smurfblossom rolled the word around on her tongue. "Papa, Papa, Paaaaapaaaaa!" Feeling satisfied that she got it right, and also that he was the bad guy, she raised her stick, preparing to charge at him.

"Smurfblossom! No!" Smurfwillow shouted.

Smurflily stepped in and snatched Smurfblossom's stick away.

"Oh, come on! Just give me one good hit!" Smurfblossom was all wound up.

"Breathe deep and step away from the Papa thing," Smurfwillow told her.

Smurfette stood next to Papa and introduced him. "Everyone ... meet Papa Smurf."

Excited whispers filled the air as the girls surrounded Papa, pulling on his beard and poking at him. They were talking so fast, he couldn't always see who was saying what:

"Hi."

"I'm Smurfjade."

"How old are you?"

"Are you a wizard?"

"What's that thing on your face?"

"How does it stay on?"

Papa's head was spinning so he pushed away from them, to get some air. "There's so many ... " He leaned over to Smurfette and asked her, "Where are the boys?"

Hefty, Clumsy, and Brainy stepped forward. They knew they were in big trouble.

Hefty kicked the dirt, not wanting to make eye contact. "'Sup, Papa."

Brainy looked down too. "Hello there."

Only Clumsy was excited to see Papa. He blurted out, "I rode Spitfire!"

Papa was angry that they'd left the village, but he was also glad to see them. "Well, thank goodness you're all okay."

Papa then turned to Smurfwillow. Finding out that there were other female Smurfs ... This was the biggest surprise of his long life.

⋆ The Lost Village ⋆

"How did you find us?" Smurfette asked. She hadn't left any clues to where she was going.

"I, uh, wasn't born yesterday, you know," he told her, which made Smurfwillow laugh.

"That's clear," she said as a small joke.

Papa ignored her, telling his Smurfs, "Look. You four are coming home with me. Now." He pointed to the waiting Bucky.

"Not so fast, Papa thing." Smurfwillow blocked his way.

"Papa thi—? I— Are you the one in charge around here?" He was insulted.

"That's right," she said. "I'm Smurfwillow. Leader of the Smurfs."

"Well, I'm afraid that's quite impossible, because I happen to be the leader of the Smurfs, so—"

Smurfwillow rolled her eyes. "Whatever you say, Papa thing."

Papa was trying his best to be civil, but she was making him mad. "Excuse me? Do you mind not calling me that?"

"Well, if the thing fits ... " Smurfwillow was still standing directly in front of Papa. The two of them stared at each other, hard.

Finally, Papa asked, "By the way. Where'd you learn those moves?"

"Self taught, actually," she said, not turning her gaze.

"Impressive." Papa gave a small nod.

"Thank you," she replied.

Chapter 12 Gargamel Attacked the Smurfy Grove

"You're quite welcome."

They smiled slightly to each other and then bowed. None of the Smurfs in the grove understood what was going on between them.

Smurfette cut in, asking, "Okay, not sure what's happening here, but, uh, what about Gargamel?"

"Now what's all this nonsense about Garga—?" Papa started when all of a sudden there was a BOOM!

And a FLASH!

When the burst of green smoke cleared, Papa and Smurfwillow were stuck like statues. They'd been hit by one of Gargamel's Freeze Balls!

"Gargamel!" Smurfette shouted, looking around frantically. Where was he hiding?

"Oh, I'm sorry, did I scare you?" Gargamel chuckled, stepping out into the open. "I hope so."

He grabbed Papa Smurf and Smurfwillow and threw them into a sack.

Smurfette called out, "Everybody, run!"

That made Gargamel laugh even harder. There would be no escape. "Prepare for Garmageddon!" he told them all.

POUNCE! Azrael crashed through the grove, blocking their path, while Monty zoomed overhead. The bird pushed anyone who wanted to leave back toward Azrael.

* The Lost Village *

They were trapped.

Smurfs took off in every direction, running for whatever cover they could find.

"Spears, now!" Smurfstorm commanded.

Some of the girls got ready to throw spears at Gargamel, but the wizard wasn't scared. "Gargamel says 'freeze'!" he shouted, blowing freeze powder on the attacking Smurfs.

Gargamel clapped with joy when the Smurfs stopped moving. "That's right! Smurf tested, Gargamel approved, grade A, first-class high-octane Freeze Balls!"

He attacked again, and this time Smurfstorm was frozen.

"Freeze Ball! Freeze Ball! Freeze Ball!" Gargamel chanted as he tossed them at the Smurfs.

"Meow, meow, meow!" Azrael complained.

"Well, I assume they'll still work if I don't shout 'Freeze Ball'," Gargamel explained. "But we'll never know." He tossed another toward a group of fleeing Smurfs. "Freeze Ball!"

Monty helped Gargamel with an aerial attack, dropping Freeze Balls from overhead.

Smurfette tried desperately to save her new friends. She dashed from Smurf to Smurf, trying to shake them out of it.

Gargamel took aim directly at Smurfette, but Hefty jumped in front

Chapter 12 Gargamel Attacked the Smurfy Grove

of her. "Smurfette!"

Hefty was frozen.

"Hefty?!" Smurfette tried to break the spell while Gargamel tossed dozens of stunned Smurfs into his sack.

"It's. Over. Smurfette." Hefty struggled to get out each word.

Gargamel was thrilled, dancing around, scooping up Smurfs as though he were putting jelly beans into a jar.

Azrael held open the bag. "Meow!"

Gargamel called to the bird, "Monty! Bag o' Smurfs!"

Monty swooped down and picked up the sack with his beak.

Smurfette was the only one not frozen. She desperately tried to break Hefty free of his stun spell. Or Brainy. Or Clumsy. Anybody.

Hefty mumbled through frozen lips, "It's time. For you. To run."

As he finished, Gargamel snatched Hefty and Brainy.

"NO!" Smurfette shrieked.

"Two more for pick up!" Gargamel tossed Brainy and Hefty into the air, and Monty scooped them up. The bird headed into the darkness. Gargamel laughed. "Ha, ha, ha, ha, ha!"

Smurfette was devastated.

Gargamel turned around to face her. "Ah, Smurfette, my little creation!" he cooed. "You finally did what you were made for."

"No, it's not true," She cried, refusing to believe him.

* The Lost Village *

"Of course it is! Why do you think you led me here? Why did you save me on the river?" He gave her a wicked grin. "It was all part of the plan. No matter how hard you try, you can't escape your destiny. But now you're really of no use to me anymore." He reached into his bag, said "Freeze Ball", then tossed his last one at her.

Smurfette was frozen and helpless.

"Thank you for everything," Gargamel told her, then grabbed the last of the girl Smurfs.

Smurfblossom, with tears in her eyes, fought to say, "Smurfette, how could you do this to us?"

Gargamel grabbed her and said, "Because it was her purpose!" And then he took off.

Smurfette was stuck: frozen and all alone.

It was over.

Smurfy Grove was empty.

Gargamel had captured all the Smurfs.

And it was all Smurfette's fault.

Chapter 13 Smurfette Saved Smurfs (1)

When the freezing spell wore off, Smurfette crumbled to the ground. She was scared. Her tears turned to sobs just as rain began to fall.

Gargamel never froze Brainy's Snappy Bug, but in the fighting, he got flipped over on his back. He wiggled and squirmed his way back onto his feet and scurried over to Smurfette. Snappy Bug was worried. In an attempt to lift Smurfette's spirits, he drew a heart in the mud, but that only made Smurfette cry harder.

The Dragonfly Spitfire rested nearby. He was also worried about Smurfette.

Out of the darkness, Bucky appeared in the clearing.

Smurfette looked up through her tears and said, "Huh?"

Snappy Bug jumped at the opportunity to show Smurfette something to cheer her up. She quickly printed the smurfy selfie of Smurfette and the boys around the campfire, in much happier times.

Smurfette gazed at the selfie, longing for her friends. Then she turned away. "I'm sorry, you guys ... " She was too sad to think about anything.

Snappy Bug nuzzled against her, giving her a bug hug. Spitfire and Bucky joined them. Bucky gave her a little nudge, as if to say, "You can

* The Lost Village *

do it. Go get them!"

Smurfette sighed. "No, Snappy. I've done too much damage already."

Snappy played a recording of their journey. It started with Hefty's voice: "We're Team Smurf, and we're in this together."

Then Smurfette was heard: "We're Smurfs. We do the right thing."

Smurfette thought about the recoding, their journey, and everything that had happened.

"I'm not even a real Smurf," she cried. Then she stopped crying, as though she'd realized something. "I'm not a real Smurf!"

Suddenly, she jumped up, grabbed Snappy Bug, and climbed onto Bucky's back.

They took off!

At Gargamel's lair, the sky was dark and ominous. It was raining. Thunder crashed. Lightning lit up the sky.

"We need more power!" The wizard called to Monty.

Gargamel pulled a lever on a giant contraption. "Faster, Monty, faster! Yes."

A cookie dropped in front of Monty, who was running on a treadmill that powered the machine. Monty ran as fast as his little bird legs could handle while Gargamel inspected the different parts of the machine.

Chapter 13 Smurfette Saved Smurfs (1)

"The jiggler is jiggling. The spin-y thing is spinning. The smoke is going up." It was working! "The bubblers are bubbling. Hubbuda, hubbuda! Perfect!"

All the power flowed into a clear fishbowl-shaped centrifuge. It began to swirl and bubble.

Gargamel examined the bowl with glee. "Ooooh! It's almost there."

The Smurfs were trapped in cages hanging from the rafters. In one cage, Brainy attempted to pick the lock with his hand while Hefty and Smurfstorm waited, hoping he could free them.

"Here's what we're going to do," Brainy said. "I pick this lock ... "

"Yeah?" Hefty, Clumsy, and Smurfstorm chorused.

"We swing to that shelf ... " Brainy pointed out a shelf on the far side of the room.

"Yeah?"

"Pick up something heavy ... "

"Yeah?"

"And use it to kill the bird!" Brainy finished.

"Wait! You want us to kill the bird?!" Hefty asked incredulously.

"Fine," Brainy conceded. "We'll just knock him unconscious."

The others agreed to this plan while Smurfstorm made some hand signals to Smurfwillow, who was in another cage with Papa. "They have an escape plan. But they're going to need our help."

⋆ The Lost Village ⋆

"It's time to rock the cage," Papa said.

Smurfwillow gave him a look. "Don't be weird."

Across the room, Brainy gave the lock one more twist and *click*! It opened. They all lined hands and leaped from the cages. Hefty held on as they swung over to the next cage like trapeze artists. Papa and Smurfwillow grabbed hold, and they continued to form links with their hands. "Gotcha!" Smurfwillow shouted.

Azrael spotted them and meowed to get Gargamel's attention, "MEOW! MEOW!!!"

Gargamel scowled at his cat. "Stop that, Azrael! I can't calibrate my machine with all your incessant yammering!"

Papa and Smurfwillow, meanwhile, swung the Smurfs over to the nearby shelf, making a chain with Hefty and Clumsy at its front. Gargamel turned and saw the string of Smurfs that were practically free. "Sweet mercy! It's another jailbreak! Azrael! You're completely useless." With that, the wizard swooped them up in his net, breaking the chain and leaving Hefty and Brainy alone on the shelf. "Lucky for you I have eyes in the back of my head."

"No, Gargamel! No!" Papa yelled.

"Quiet down! You'll all get your turn! In you go!" Gargamel dumped the Smurfs from his net into the centrifuge, and they started to spin, the color draining from them as the spun around.

Chapter 13 Smurfette Saved Smurfs (1)

Gargamel was completely focused on the spinning centrifuge, studying the fluid closely as its color began to glow brighter. A blue mist rose up from the centrifuge and flowed into the machine. Gargamel smiled and turned a handle; the magic descended upon him in a glowing display.

Smurfwillow and Papa rattled the bars of their cage. "NOOOOOO!"

"Yes! That's the stuff! Ha, ha, ha! It's working! I can feel it! I can feel the power!" Gargamel used his new power to give himself a wizard makeover, starting with his robe.

"Oh-ho, ho, ho, ho!" New clean robes appeared. Next, he touched his head and ZAAAAP! A full head of luxurious hair grew.

"Ha, ha, ha! Check out my wizard mane!" Gargamel shook his long hair delightedly.

"When I'm through with these Smurfs, I'll have all the power I've ever dreamed of!"

Smurfette stepped out of the shadows. "Almost all the power!"

Hefty ran to one side of the cage. "Smurfette!" he cried out.

Gargamel's grin grew. "Smurfette?! What a lovely surprise. Are you done crying in the woods?" He zapped a bolt of energy at her.

She slid down a curtain. "I've shed enough tears for these Smurfs!"

Gargamel looked at her with interest. "What's this?"

Smurfette continued, "I'm done pretending to be something I'm not. I've come to repledge my loyalty to you! My true papa!"

Chapter 14 Smurfette Saved Smurfs (2)

Papa and Smurfwillow were watching Smurfette from their cage.

"She can't be serious?" Smurfwillow asked Papa.

"No, no, no," Papa assured her. "She would never!"

"Oh Smurfette," Gargamel said. "Even if I did believe you—which I don't!—what could you possibly offer me that I don't already have? A tiny little massage that I can't even feel?"

Smurfette had her answer ready. "How about the rest of the Smurfs?"

Gargamel laughed as if she'd just told him the funniest joke. "Yeah, right." Then he considered her offer. "Wait, what?"

"Just think of all the power you'll have once I reveal the location of Smurf Village," she told him.

Gargamel was suddenly interested. "Let's see, now ... One hundred more Smurfs ... That's ten times the power. No, sixteen times the ... Let's see, carry the one ... " He gave up on doing the math. "Whatever! It's a lot more power! Now, why are you doing this?"

"I'm so tired of being good," Smurfette said. "Use your power to transform me back to my evil self."

Chapter 14 Smurfette Saved Smurfs (2)

"Your loyalty has returned to you." The wizard was pleased.

"So do we have a deal?" Smurfette asked.

The Smurfs in cages gasped. Papa yelled, "Smurfette, no!"

"Quiet, you vile blue rats, I'm thinking! Okay, I'm done! Let's do it!" Gargamel let his power build and threw every bit of it at her. "One evil Smurfette, coming right up!" He zapped her with power and held the magical beam steady.

Smurfette focused on the power and began to emit a bright light. The glow acted like a force field against the magic. It was taking all her strength to stay steady.

Hefty and Brainy watched, uncertain of what she was doing, when Brainy said, "Wait! Of course!"

"Wait!" Gargamel realized something was wrong. "What's happening? No! No! What are you doing?!"

"Yeah!" Brainy and Hefty cheered. "Go, Smurfette!"

Gargamel's head of thick hair faded away. His robes were reduced back to their original form. His hovel began to fall apart. The machine sparked, overloaded, and shattered.

As the magic deflected off Smurfette, blue coloring returned to the first Smurfs who had gone into the machine.

"NOOOOOOOOO!" Gargamel shouted.

The Smurfs hooted and hollered in celebration.

⋆ The Lost Village ⋆

"Azrael!" Gargamel called to his cat. "Help!! More power!" Azrael ran to the machine faucet to turn it, hoping to replenish the wizard's power.

Brainy turned to Hefty. "What are we going to do?"

Hefty spotted a spoon and got an idea. Grabbing Brainy's arm, he pulled him in. "We smurfboard!"

They grabbed the spoon and leaped off the shelf. Together, they smurfboarded down an ax handle, jumped onto a wooden ramp, and launched themselves at Gargamel's bird Monty. Shouting "TEAM SMURF!" they knocked out Monty, landed, and skidded to a stop. The machine, meanwhile, started sparking and overloading, and then shut down.

A magical tempest began to swirl around the room. As it grew stronger, it shot Gargamel, Azrael, and Monty through the roof!

"Nooooo!" Gargamel screamed as he went flying.

All the Smurfs cheered and shouted Smurfette's name. They hugged one another and danced to celebrate. The Smurfs were saved!

The Smurfs still in cages were set free. They climbed down ladders into the room. The ones in the cauldron woke up to discover their color and magic had returned.

"I'm okay! Yeah!" Clumsy said as Hefty and Brainy helped him up.

"I thought we were goners," Smurfblossom said, embracing her

Chapter 14 Smurfette Saved Smurfs (2)

friends.

"Okay, everybody's ... Thanks goodness," Smurfwillow said, sighing with relief.

"I can't believe she did it!" Brainy said, looking around.

"Where's Smurfette?" Hefty noticed they hadn't seen her.

Smurfette was on a ledge a few feet away, but something wasn't right. As the Smurfs approached, they realized that Gargamel's magic had returned her to her original form—a clay mold of a girl Smurf. She lay in a heap on the ground. The selfie of her and her friends lay next to her.

"Smurfette?" Hefty didn't understand. Was this really her?

Papa Smurf fell to his knees, tears filling his eyes.

Hefty asked, "What happened?" As he said it, his heart ached with sadness.

Papa Smurf explained, "This is what she once was."

All the Smurfs were stunned and very, very sad.

Smurfblossom burst into tears.

Brainy stood there, unable to think for the first time in his life. He felt cold inside.

Suddenly, Papa jumped up and started flipping through Gargamel's spell book. "There has to be something I can do!" He muttered to himself as he flipped pages, "There must be a spell or ... Where is it? What page? Must be here ... No, that's not it. Which spell? Which spell?"

⋆ The Lost Village ⋆

The Smurfs watched, feeling powerless. There was no way to help.

Papa anxiously flipped through Gargamel's spell book, searching for an answer.

The Smurfs had tears in their eyes watching Papa. He was desperate to save his little girl.

Brainy stepped forward. "Papa," he said softly. "We won't find the answer to this in a book."

Papa knew that Brainy was right. He slammed the book to the ground, angry and frustrated.

Hefty cradled the clay Smurfette in his arms. "Let's take her home."

Chapter 15 Gathered in Smurf Village

All the Smurfs, boys and girls, escorted Smurfette home. The woods were peaceful after the rains. Wind whistled through the trees, and the night stars provided a soft glow.

Smurfette's clay form lay in the middle of a circle formed by the Smurfs. The entire village took turns placing flowers and gifts near her, including the selfie of her and the boys.

Papa Smurf stood before the others and said, "Smurfette never believed she was a real Smurf, but she was the truest Smurf of all."

Brainy removed his glasses to wipe his tears. Snappy Bug climbed onto his shoulder. The bug was also crying.

Hefty placed a small bluebell flower on the clay form, holding back his tears.

Clumsy joined his brothers. He took Hefty's hand. The Smurfs began taking one another's hands, until a chain of two hundred Smurfs, from both the village and the grove, surrounded Smurfette.

The wind picked up, and the moon shone brightly, peeking out from behind the clouds.

After a few moments, Smurfs began to break away from the circle

* The Lost Village *

to head back to their mushrooms. At last, the only three remaining were Hefty, Brainy, and Clumsy. They stood together, eyes closed, holding hands, bonded forever.

They didn't notice it, but the bluebell flower resting on the clay form began to sparkle.

Slowly but surely, blue light seeped into Smurfette's clay form. Life began to return to her. Smurfette's nose wiggled. Her hair shone golden. And finally, she opened her eyes.

She sat up. "Why is everyone crying?"

Clumsy still had his eyes closed when he responded. "It's Smurfette. She's a lump of clay."

Smurfette stepped close. "No, Clumsy, it's me. I'm right here."

Clumsy looked up to see Smurfette. He grabbed her nose to make sure she was real, then, once convinced he announced, "Smurfette?! It's Smurfette!"

Brainy and Hefty were still in the moment with their eyes closed.

"Quiet, Clumsy," Brainy said.

"Let him be, Brainy. We all grieve in our own way," Hefty said, having returned.

"Clumsy, would you—Oh ... " Brainy saw Smurfette standing there.

She was awake! The boys all rushed to her side.

Their celebration was so loud that the other Smurfs came running

Chapter 15 Gathered in Smurf Village

back. Papa Smurf was more stunned than anyone. She laughed and hugged him tight.

"Look at you. You never cease to amaze me," Papa said. They held each other for a long moment.

When Smurfblossom found out what had happened, she rushed forward, barreling into Smurfette. Then the others joined her, surrounding Smurfette with love and hugs.

Papa Smurf sat in his comfortable chair in his mushroom house. A book lay open on his lap. "Hey, there ... Me again. Kind of a wild ride, wasn't it? But in the end, Smurfette found her purpose and united us all."

All two hundred Smurfs were working side by side.

"Let's get two lead welders up on the top!" Handy Smurf called. Smurfette jumped onto a roof with another Smurf.

Clumsy tried to help, but he ended up just tripping. "I'm okay!"

Papa said, "Every Smurf pitched in. We all worked together to rebuild Smurfy Grove, bigger and better than ever."

Smurfwillow and Papa Smurf continued to fight, but now in a ring, with Smurf judges.

"From that day forward, both villages had an open-door policy, and I'm happy to report we see one another often," Papa reported.

Papa Smurf practiced some steps Smurfwillow taught him.

⋆ The Lost Village ⋆

"Pretty good, for an old-timer." Smurfwillow gave him a pat on the back.

"You're not bad yourself," Papa replied with a laugh.

Smurfette helped Brainy in the lab and Baker in the kitchen.

Papa went on reading from his book. "And as for that burning question, what exactly is a Smurfette? Well, it's just a name. It doesn't define her. Smurfette can be whatever she wants to be. But don't take my word for it ... "

"What's a Smurfette?" Brainy asked. "Well, I don't need a book to tell you she's—"

"Beeedeeebeeedeeebeee," Snappy interrupted.

"Yes, Snappy, I know. That's exactly what I was going to—"

"Beeedeeebeeedeeebeee," Snappy cut in again.

"Well, if you'd let me finish—"

"Beeedeeebeeedeeebeee."

"Right. Smurfette can't be defined by just one word. She's many things."

"She doesn't know it yet, but she's my new best friend!" Smurfblossom added.

"Smurfette is fearless," Clumsy put in.

"Hmm, well, why don't you tell me what *you* know first," Nosey said.

Chapter 15 Gathered in Smurf Village

Hefty catapulted Nosey Smurf into the distance. "Smurfette is everything. And more."

"She's tough," Smurfstorm said. "Not as tough as me, but tough."

Paranoid Smurf quickly pulled down the shade and refused to answer.

"Smurfette is a true leader," Smurfwillow put in.

Papa Smurf smiled. "She shines!"

Baker Smurf had one thing to say. "She still stinks at baking!"

Smurfette sat on a bench, watching the usual goings-on in Smurf Village. Everything was back to normal. Jazzy Smurf played his music in the center of town. Grouchy walked up and sat beside her.

"Hey! I'm grouchin' here," Smurfette told him with a frown.

Grouchy was shocked and slinked away.

Smurfette laughed. "Just kidding!"

Grouchy came back, a bit confused, and took his place on his bench. He was really grumpy. "Why don't you go and Smurfette somewhere else?!"

Smurfette flashed him a sweet smile.

"Or, uh ... I g-guess you can Smurfette right here," he stammered.

Smurfette gave him a big hug. "That's exactly what I intend to do!"

Smurfette bounced away, happy and cheerful.

∗ The Lost Village ∗

Grouchy watched her go, privately smiling to himself.

All the Smurfs gathered in the center of town. Snappy Bug was ready for them.

"Come on, everyone! Smurfy selfie time!" Smurfette stood in the middle of her two hundred best friends.

All the Smurfs smiled and in one voice said:

"BLUE CHEESE!"